PARENTING A HIGHLY SENSITIVE CHILD

MASTERING PRACTICAL STRATEGIES TO
OVERCOME THE CHALLENGES OF RAISING
HIGHLY SENSITIVE CHILDREN. UNLOCKING THEIR
POTENTIAL FOR SUCCESS IN AN
OVERWHELMING WORLD

ALISON CRAWFORD

CONTENTS

INTRODUCTION

Highly sensitive children see the world differently. Their experience of emotions and sensations is completely different and deeply intensive, which is not always understood by the people around them. Therefore, they are easily overwhelmed and often overreact. Parents should understand their child's unique gifts and treat them accordingly.

The book begins by explaining the concept of high sensitivity in children and the different factors that affect their nature. You'll get some insight into the origin of high sensitivity and learn its different characteristics so you can recognize them in your child. Next, you will learn about emotional intelligence and its connection with high sensitivity. You can also use practical strategies to encourage this quality in your child.

The home environment plays a huge role in the life of a highly sensitive child. The book sets out strategies on how to create a nurturing and supportive home catering to your child's unique needs and making them feel safe and secure.

Highly sensitive children struggle with communication. Parents should provide a safe space for their children to express themselves. The book sets you up with various techniques to validate their feelings and handle their communication needs.

Your child can easily be overwhelmed and often experience anxiety. There are several tips in this book to equip them with the right tools to cope with their emotions.

The world can be harsh for a highly sensitive child with low self-esteem, and they can struggle in their daily lives. You can use various techniques to build their resilience and boost their self-esteem, so they can navigate social situations with strength and compassion.

Schools can provide your highly sensitive child with either opportunities or challenges. The book discusses them both in detail and can advise on effective and practical methods to choose the right school environment for them and to support their education.

Your highly sensitive child will have different needs at every stage of their life. The book will guide you through them by detailing several approaches to dealing with your child's needs until adolescence.

Highly sensitive children also struggle with maintaining healthy social skills. You will discover practical strategies to foster your child's communication and social skills.

The book explains the significance of academic success for your highly sensitive child and what you can do to accommodate their learning style and support their educational journey. The last chapter focuses on you and your needs. Parenting a highly sensitive child isn't easy. Parents shouldn't neglect self-care and seek support when they need it. You will learn helpful tips to take care of yourself and your needs.

This book provides you with all the information you need to care for a highly sensitive child with effective and practical methods and techniques to provide a safe and comforting environment for them.

UNDERSTANDING HIGHLY SENSITIVE CHILDREN

This chapter delves deep into the concept of high sensitivity in children, what it means, and the biological and environmental factors that contribute to a child's sensitivity, and gives you a chance to understand why children with this condition need additional guidance throughout their development. Moreover, knowing the signs and characteristics of high sensitivity will help you understand your child's needs.

What It Means to Be Highly Sensitive

In common parlance, being highly sensitive is defined as experiencing emotions more profoundly and too often. Extra-sensitive individuals have ferocious emotional, physical, and cognitive responses to internal or external stimuli. This is believed to be the consequence of differences in brain development in early childhood, which causes a broad range of symptoms and difficulties throughout the person's life. High sensitivity is more commonly associated with introverted personalities, although those with extrovert character traits can also face these issues.

While it's not considered a disorder or condition, it's estimated that one in five people have certain degrees of heightened sensitivity to sensory stimuli.

Overly sensitive individuals are classified as neurodivergent, which means their nervous system works differently from the brain of neurotypicals. While these individuals are often criticized for their traits and socially unacceptable behavior, they also have their strengths.

Extra-sensitive individuals are often labeled "too sensitive." Yet, they think those who invalidate their sensitivity are insensitive and cruel. While their inability to cope with stimuli causes them to become emotionally, mentally, and sometimes physically overwhelmed, it's critical to remember that high sensitivity isn't an illness. The behaviors involved with it can be treated. If your child has heightened responsiveness to negative and positive stimuli, you can help them refine the skills that modify these reactions.

Biological and Environmental Factors That Contribute to a Child's Sensitivity

What makes a child highly sensitive depends on a number of factors, including genetics, environment, early childhood experiences, and developmental challenges. It might come as a surprise, but high sensitivity is not an exclusively human trait. Many animals have it and use it as a survival tool for escaping predators and other dangers in their environment. However, unlike animals, people have another component to this trait - emotions. People are equipped with a level of emotional intelligence that allows them to decide when to apply their heightened sensory skills. However, some people lack the ability to do that, remaining on guard, even when there isn't any immediate danger, and effectively relinquishing emotional control. The same happens when a child can't switch off the parts of their brain responsible for analyzing and processing stimuli. They remain in a state of constant excitement and focus, which results in anxiety.

One of the reasons children become highly sensitive might lie in their parent's inability to notice the symptoms early and help their kids overcome them. Parents often think their child is just going through a sensitive phase but will eventually "grow out of it." Unfortunately, it isn't this simple. If a child experiences heightened sensitivity to external or internal stimuli in early childhood and doesn't receive the necessary help to cope in a healthy way, their brain learns that it needs to remain alert and in control. However, this isn't the only contributing factor. Children often began to display signs of high sensitivity after a negative experience. Likewise, genetics also play a significant part in developing high sensitivity. Children whose parents are more susceptible to stimuli will more than likely become sensitive themselves. Moreover, several genes associated with sensitivity are activated only after a traumatic experience. In this case, the child is born with the potential to be susceptible to stimuli, but whether they acquire these traits depends on their early childhood experiences.

Lastly, neurodevelopmental factors also contribute to a child's sensitivity. Specifically, the most prominent role belongs to the development of the dopamine system. Dopamine is a chemical released by the nervous system and influences people's personalities, moods, and behaviors. It's responsible for the fight or flight response you experience in potentially dangerous situations. Children with high sensitivity to stimuli have much higher dopamine levels, which causes them to be anxious more frequently than their peers. Dopamine is a neurotransmitter (a chemical subject to transmitting information through the nervous system), and excess dopamine leads to a constant state of hyperawareness. Consequently, children with high dopamine levels will have too many thoughts and emotions to deal with. Dopamine is also known as the feel-good hormone because it's released as a reward for something the brain finds conducive in any shape or form. In children, an excess level of dopamine causes an unhealthy balance in this reward system, making them crave the reward by staying in control all the time.

The Origin and Nature of High Sensitivity

Albeit a relatively new concept, sensitivity is getting more and more attention in psychology. While science still has plenty of areas to uncover when it comes to this personality trait, researchers have learned a lot about it over the past three decades.

The concept of high sensitivity was first introduced by Elaine Aron (the author of the book The Highly Sensitive Person) and Arthur Aron in the mid-1990s. Despite the lukewarm reception at the time, interest in the topic has grown steadily and has even picked up pace in recent years. That said, the roots of sensitivity can be traced back to a much earlier researcher - the works of Carl Jung, a renowned psychiatrist who studied innate sensitivity over 100 years ago. After noticing that some people are inherently sensitive to stimuli and, thus, unable to control their responses, Jung (and later his successors) began to investigate the trait. Soon after, scientists began associating sensitivity with behavior inhibition and, later, introverted personality traits. However, it was only near the last century that studies began to focus on sensitivity as a standalone trait. Soon after, several new theories arose, and research intensified.

One of the first theories of sensitivity was formed by Elaine and Art Arn, who named the trait Sensory Processing Sensitivity (SPS). It was a fundamental milestone in sensitivity research because it represented a stepping stone for empirical research to test sensitivity-related theories. The SPS theory research was geared towards adults and helped researchers sort out which behaviors are - and which aren't related to sensitivity. The second prominent theory was the Biological Sensitivity to Context (BSC), developed by Bruce Elli and Tom Boyce, who researched the effects of psychological stress in children. This involved longitudinal research - the kind that follows individuals over a certain period. Seeing how children reacted to stressors from a young age gave researchers profound insights into what sensitive children need to thrive. The third theory, Differential Susceptibility (DS) by Jay Belsky, was similarly oriented as it focused on the susceptibility of infants to negative stimuli. It proved that some youngsters are more intensely affected by negative experiences than others.

A critical early development that arose from these three studies was a self-applied measure of sensitivity called the Highly Sensitive Person Scale. Through this, adults and older children can learn how sensitive they are by answering a set of simple questions. This paved the way for additional studies investigating how sensitivity was related to other characteristics. This was crucial because, for the first time, scientists were able to distinguish sensitivity from introversion. Moreover, after testing the three main (and several follow-up) theories, researchers gained more knowledge about the concept of sensitivity as part of the human personality and its connection to brain functions and the genetics of sensitivity.

The next logical step was to research the abovementioned connection - which is exactly what scientists did in the past 10 years. First, they developed the theory of environmental sensitivity - the concept that refines how professionals view sensitivity. Essentially, it meant that all three early theories were mashed together, creating a better framework for understanding the effects of the environment on children's sensitivity.

More empirical investigation followed, and research broadened to seek a deeper understanding of the psychological, physiological, and genetic segments of sensitivity. As a result, new, more efficient ways of measuring sensitivity in children and adolescents were devised. Instead of their assessment being based on the parents' observation, kids were now observed by trained behavioral experts. This led to further breakthroughs.

Up to this point, psychologists were only able to differentiate between two groups of people: those who were highly sensitive and those who were not. However, research involving larger groups showed that sensitivity shows a continuum. In other words, there are many levels of sensitivity, and being overly sensitive and not being sensitive are just the two ends of the spectrum. Everyone has some level of sensitivity, and some express this trait more profoundly than others.

Psychologists nowadays divide individuals into three groups based on their sensitivity to make a diagnosis and provide guidance and assistance more streamlined. Those with low sensitivity can thrive in any environment and aren't affected by negative experiences. Those with medium sensitivity are somewhat less resilient than the previous group and have more weaknesses when it comes to distress tolerance and emotional regulation. Lastly, the third group is composed of individuals with high sensitivity. They require tightly controlled conditions to flourish, but when their needs are met, they can thrive and become balanced and happy adults.

Another breakthrough was the discovery that sensitivity has its own personality profile. At first, researchers thought that sensitivity was an underlying trait associated with other characteristics like a lack of openness to new experiences, neuroticism, etc. In other words, those open to new ideas are more creative while managing their emotions. Since then, it has been discovered that personality is a standalone trait - although it can appear along with other characteristics and unhealthy coping mechanisms. Therefore, if a child is extra-sensitive, their emotions can get out of control whether they enjoy new experiences or not. However, it's been proven that over time, the excess of negative triggers can lead to avoidance of previously enjoyed or new experiences.

Lastly, researchers discovered that the characteristic of sensitivity is encoded in several different genes. These genes are responsible for the function of several brain regions, including the amygdala and the hippocampus (both of which play crucial roles in sensitivity). This proved that sensitive children were inherently born that way. However, further research has established that several genetic factors must come together across the entire genetic makeup for an individual to express sensitivity.

Signs and Characteristics of High Sensitivity in Children

Overly sensitive children often display a unique set of characteristics. While not all sensitive kids possess all of these traits (and those who aren't as susceptible to external stimuli can also struggle with these issues), noticing them in your child could be an indicator that they're more sensitive than usual.

Their Emotions Can Be Extreme

Children who are more susceptible to emotional triggers experience emotions more profoundly than their peers. They can go from laughing with infectious joy to screaming in rage in a matter of seconds. When they experience negative emotions, their words and actions will become extremely irrational as well. For example, if your child gets upset because they can't play with their favorite toy at lunchtime, they will say they'll never eat what you give them again (or refuse to eat if they can't express themselves verbally).

Their Reactions to Sensory Input Are Exaggerated

Extra-sensitive kids aren't triggered only by their emotions. In fact, smells, sights, textures, tastes, and sounds can be even more overwhelming to their senses. Each sensory input registers in their brain more intensely, causing them to react when confronted by a specific trigger. For example, your child might refuse to eat their food because they hate how it smells or tastes or go into a rage when they're forced to wear clothes with a texture they don't like. Your child might also refuse to go to noisy places because they're too overwhelmed by the sounds. Conversely, they'll be more aware of their surroundings and immediately notice something out of place or unusual. As soon as they perceive something isn't as it ought to be, their mind is bombarded with warning signs, triggering intense, emotion-amplifying thoughts.

They Can Have a Meltdown over the Smallest Things

Meltdowns in children are caused by stress and the accompanying negative emotions. Because highly sensitive kids are more affected by stress, their meltdowns will be triggered more quickly. They can get stressed out over paltry issues (like the inability to wear certain clothes) all the time. Consequently, their temper rises very frequently. They're overwhelmed by far more stimuli than other kids, which shows in the high prevalence of their intense meltdowns.

Their Brain Never Stops Processing

Sensitive children have an overactive brain, which keeps their focus sharp, and their need to analyze and process what's happening around them in full gear. Besides their keen spatial awareness, these kids are also tuned into other people. They can detect slight nuances in your tone when you're talking to them and everyone else. For example, if your child notices you got upset while talking to someone on the phone, they'll immediately come to you and try to "help you" any way they can. While this makes them empathetic and insightful, the ability to absorb all this information often overwhelms them.

They Want to Control Everything

Sensitive kids like to know what's happening around them all the time, which gives them a sense of control. Their mind will conjure distinct ideas of how things should be to maintain control and avoid situations when intense emotions are triggered. Dictating occurrences, like the color of their bowl, where they and others sit, and how close certain items can be on the table, makes it easier to manage their feelings. At the same time, their ideas can be incredibly rigid. When their expectations aren't met, the tight control over their emotions slips, causing a meltdown. Moreover, their need to control everything in their outer world only masks the inability to control what's happening in their inner world.

They're Extremely Cautious

Children more susceptible to external stimuli are also more fearful and cautious in unfamiliar situations. When they encounter these situations, their brain's processing functions go into overdrive. They don't know what types of stimuli they can expect. They become worried about what will happen, who they'll encounter, what others expect from them, whether they'll be liked or safe, and a myriad of other aspects. Although their cautious nature can make your child seem bright and insightful (and make you think they'll be safe), it can often overwhelm them. When your child knows they'll be expected to face new situations (like a new classroom in a higher grade or their friend's upcoming birthday party), they might feel anxious for the day ahead. To keep control and stay in their comfort zone, they might try to avoid these situations by refusing to leave your side when you arrive at the place where the worrisome event will take place. Because of this, sensitive children need more time to adapt when they start nursery, preschool, or sports activities (which they coincidentally like - they just don't like that it takes place in an unfamiliar environment).

They Get Frustrated Very Easily

Extra-sensitive children have a very low threshold for distress tolerance. They get frustrated more easily in stressful situations. Whenever they're confronted with a challenge, they become upset with their inability to cope with their emotions and tend to give up trying altogether. While all children experience some level of discomfort when trying to use a skill they just started to learn, this feeling reaches new heights for a sensitive child. For example, if they can't make a block tower stand after their second try, they will give up crying rather than try again and figure out how to prevent the blocks from tumbling down.

They're Perfectionists

Overly sensitive kids don't like to lose. They want to be the best in everything because their mind tells them they should be. When things don't turn out that way, they lose control of their emotions, which causes them overwhelming discomfort. Your child might feel ashamed after failing to accomplish something they think they should've done very easily.

They Don't Like to Be Corrected

Due to their drive for control, highly sensitive children view constructive criticism and directions as an attack against their person. They also tend to develop unhealthy coping mechanisms to protect themself from criticism and all the negative emotions it can trigger. For instance, if you try to provide your child directions on how to do something they're clearly struggling with or correct them if they were doing something wrong, they might avoid your gaze, laugh awkwardly, or walk away with a sullen face.

They Take Everything Personally

Extra-sensitive kids are more self-conscious and take things personally. They can become overly preoccupied with what others think of them. Yet when the attention is directed at them, they get very squirmish. Even if you compliment their outfit or commend them for their ability to finish a task, they feel scrutinized, assessed, or even slighted. They mistake being praised for being evaluated, which creates pressure. When the pressure becomes too much to handle, they react. In addition to taking things personally, these kids might also misinterpret their people's world and behavior. It's like having a distorted filter that makes benign words and actions seem like an attack against their personality.

They Avoid Violence in Any Form

Highly sensitive children might want to avoid animated movies or books that contain parts where a character gets injured or otherwise hurt. They feel too intensely and empathize with the character, leaving them unsettled. It makes them feel like their emotions are out of control, which they want to avoid.

They Appreciate Beauty

On a more positive note, overly sensitive children are often profoundly moved by the beauty around them. Whether they see a good trait in others or a beautiful picture, it makes them feel happy, and they will show signs of appreciating it. They have an incredibly complex inner life that's often preoccupied with negative stimuli. That said, they experience plenty of positive emotions as well. Enjoying beauty in everything is their way of trying to balance negativity with positivity.

They Need a Lot of Downtime

Unlike many other children who thrive in a socially rich environment, sensitive kids need frequent downtime. They need space to be alone with their emotions and thoughts to process them. Without this, the constant input of stimuli would stunt their already precarious ability to process their feelings. For example, your child might need to spend an hour or two every day after they arrive from kindergarten or school before they can face playtime.

2

NURTURING EMOTIONAL INTELLIGENCE

Emotional intelligence, or EQ, is a type of social skill that depends on self-awareness so children can recognize other people's emotions and tune into their own. It is the ability to understand, control, and regulate emotions so they can think clearly, express themselves, interact with others, and effectively relate to the people in their life. This ability also makes you aware of other people's emotions and use this knowledge to see things from their perspective, sympathize with them, and help them find solutions to their problems. When you interpret other people's feelings, you can develop healthy relationships with them.

Many people believe that emotional intelligence is more significant than IQ since having a high EQ can influence every area of your life, strengthen your relationships, and increase your chances of success.

Emotional intelligence makes you realize that your emotions don't only affect you, but they have a huge impact on the people in your life as well.

This chapter explores the connection between EQ and high sensitivity and provides strategies to foster this unique quality in your child.

The Role of EQ in Highly Sensitive Children

Highly sensitive children often go through a rollercoaster of emotions that causes them great frustration. They don't understand their feelings, nor do they comprehend their dramatic reactions. It is as if someone else is behind the wheel, controlling them. They need emotional intelligence to make them self-aware so they can find proper ways to manage their feelings.

Emotional intelligence gives them the ability to recognize when they are worried or anxious and vocalize these emotions in a healthy manner rather than suppressing them. When they feel overwhelmed in a loud or intense environment, EQ can equip your child with the tools to separate themselves from their emotions so they can remain calm. Since highly sensitive children struggle in social situations, emotional intelligence enables them to understand how others are feeling and connect with them on a deeper level.

High Sensitivity and Emotional Intelligence

Emotional intelligence consists of four aspects:

Social connection
Establishing relationships
Self-management
Self-knowledge

Each one of them is associated with specific skills. For instance, self-knowledge is connected to self-exploration (when your child digs deep within to understand their emotions), high self-esteem, understanding one's purpose in life, and practicing self-care.

Highly sensitive children are emotionally intelligent by nature, even if they aren't aware of it. They are great listeners, highly empathetic, socially and emotionally aware, and deep thinkers. They also experience emotions differently from other people, which are all qualities associated with emotional intelligence.

Highly sensitive kids experience everything differently, including emotional intelligence.

Highly Empathetic

These children are extremely empathetic, and, just like a sponge, they can absorb the emotions, whether positive or negative, of everyone around them. When emotional intelligence is combined with high levels of empathy, your child won't just feel other people's emotions but also use the connection they developed with the other person to better understand what they are going through. As a result, they usually know what to say or how to respond in any situation. While some people can observe a situation from the outside, a highly sensitive child with high EQ can thoroughly analyze any problem and provide a unique perspective.

Great Listening Skills

A highly sensitive child doesn't only listen to what others are saying; since they are highly empathetic and emotionally intelligent, they pay attention to every word. They aren't only listening to you but also focused on how people express themselves, like the tone of voice, facial expressions, and body language, and analyzing the meaning behind them.

Your child can understand how you are feeling even if your words contradict your true emotions. For instance, you are having a bad day, and your child asks you if you are okay. You smile and tell your child that you are great. However, since they are highly sensitive, they have already picked up on your negative emotions, so they already know something is wrong. Using emotional intelligence, your child will analyze your tone of voice and body language and will understand right away that you aren't OK.

Emotional Awareness

Empathy and emotional awareness are connected as they both give your child an insight into what other people are feeling. They can use this information to make a difference in someone's life. Although your child can feel drained by absorbing negative emotions all day, emotional intelligence can turn their high sensitivity into a superpower. Since they are the only ones who can read a room, they can use this strength to tune into other people's emotions and provide help whether they are asked for it or not.

For instance, your daughter is playing with her friends, and they are all talking excitedly about celebrating Father's Day. However, she could sense strange vibes from one of her friends. He wasn't involved in the conversation and was even trying to change the subject. Now, rather than letting these negative emotions overwhelm her, she uses her high EQ and approaches her friend in private to ask if he is OK. Her friend explains that his parents are getting a divorce and that his father and mother aren't talking with each other, so he doesn't know if he will spend Father's Day with his dad or not. In this situation, your daughter will lend a sympathetic ear to her friend and can use her special gifts by saying something to make them feel better or simply giving them a hug.

Fostering Emotional Intelligence

Your highly sensitive child most likely has a high EQ. However, since they are still young and inexperienced, they can struggle with tapping into their abilities. You can foster this quality in your child and teach them how to be emotionally intelligent.

Teaching Emotional Vocabulary

Children don't usually understand their emotions since they don't have the right vocabulary to express themselves. For instance, your sons' best friend cut him off for no reason. He isn't being himself and is lashing out because he doesn't know how to communicate that he is heartbroken.

Guide your child to understand their emotions and label them. You may not understand exactly how they are feeling since they can't tell you, but you can make an assumption based on their facial expressions and how they are acting. Using the previous example, if your child looks sad or crying, you can sit with them and say, "I know that you feel disappointed and heartbroken, right?" Or if they lose a game, you can tell them, "Are you feeling angry right now?"

Whenever your child isn't feeling like themselves, use the appropriate vocabulary like painful, shy, upset, angry, sad, frustrated, etc. You can also label your child positive emotions. For instance, if they win a game, you can say, "You are very excited right now, aren't you?"

When you watch cartoons or movies together, mute the program, and ask your child to guess how each character is feeling. If they are struggling, tell them to observe the character's facial expressions and body language and make a guess. It is a nice game you can always play together when you are watching TV.

Labeling emotions is an effective technique children can use from an early age to learn to regulate their overwhelming feelings.

Modeling Healthy Emotional Expressions

Children don't always know the appropriate way to communicate their emotions, whether in private or public. Healthy ways for children to express their feelings include painting a picture or using their words by saying, "I am sad." However, it is never appropriate for children to scream, call names, or throw tantrums whenever they are upset. You can try to tell your children how to behave, but they will only follow what you do rather than what you say.

Model healthy emotional expressions for your child to teach them the proper way to express their feelings. When you experience a frustrating situation, rather than getting angry, throwing things, or yelling at people, calmly say out loud how you are feeling. For instance, if someone cuts you off while you are driving, you can say, "I feel angry at this guy for cutting me off this way." Or when your best friend brings you a nice gift from one of their trips, you can say, "I feel happy with my gift and that my friend remembered me when they were away."

If your child is emotionally intelligent, they have probably taken this quality from one of their parents. So, you have it in you to control your emotions and express yourself in a healthy manner.

Encouraging Empathy

Adults deal with different problems every day, many of which are serious, so sometimes their children's issues seem trivial in comparison. Whenever your child is angry, sad, or experiencing any intense emotions, you can be tempted to minimize or dismiss their feelings. You don't think that losing a game or their friends canceling on them warrants this dramatic reaction. However, ignoring or dismissing your child's feelings will give them the impression that their emotions are wrong or bad. Teach your child to accept all their emotions, whether negative or positive, and not be ashamed of them.

If you disapprove of their feelings, they will learn to suppress them. Suppressed emotions won't go away and often reveal themselves through nervous tics, angry behavior, or nightmares.

Whether you understand why they are sad or not, show your child empathy and sympathize with what they are feeling. For instance, you refuse to buy them an expensive toy, so they get upset and start crying. Rather than yelling at them or dismissing their feelings, say, "I also feel sad when I can't buy something I like. It is upsetting when we can't have everything we want."

No matter how your child is feeling, it is always comforting to know that their parents understand their emotions. As a result, they won't feel the need to express themselves through intense and dramatic behavior. They will not throw tantrums or yell at you because you understand what they are going through.

Your child will learn empathy from you. They will treat others the same way you treat them. If you sympathize with them and validate their emotions, they will learn to acknowledge other people's feelings even if they don't agree with them or understand what they are going through. It is one of the most effective techniques to foster emotional intelligence in your little one.

When your child feels validated, they will start to feel better as their brain releases certain chemicals that will calm them down. When you tell your child that you understand them because you experience similar situations, they will feel seen and less alone. They will think even grown-ups have problems and can be sad and disappointed as well. They will also learn to accept every aspect of their personality, even their bad side, because you embrace their negative emotions without judgment.

Healthy Coping Mechanisms

When you apply these strategies, your child will begin to be aware of their emotions. Now, they will need to learn healthy methods to deal with them. Teach them how to regulate their feelings so they can face their negative emotions, calm themselves down, and make themselves feel better. There are various skills they can learn, like breathing exercises, affirmations, or simple meditation techniques. You can also prepare a basket for them and include their favorite comfort toy, soothing music, coloring books, and crayons, and decorate the basket with nice colors. Whenever they feel sad or angry, tell them to use any of the items in the basket to soothe themselves.

Foster Problem-Solving Skills

Fostering emotional intelligence in your child requires teaching them problem-solving skills. This step takes place after they learn emotional vocabulary and empathy. Now, they need to know how to solve their problems. For instance, if your child is sad and angry because they lost a soccer game, sit with them and calmly ask them to come up with three ways to win the game next time. Their ideas don't have to be brilliant or good; they just need to express themselves and get creative.

After they come up with three or more ideas, discuss the advantages and disadvantages of each one until they come up with the best solution for their problem.

Each time they make a mistake, ask them if there is anything they could have done to get different results. If they don't have any ideas, brainstorm together but refrain from solving their problem or giving your opinion, they should learn to do that themselves. Your child needs to see that they have the ability in them to fix their issues without any outside help. Remember, your role is only to provide guidance.

Children shouldn't give in to negative emotions but understand that there is a solution to every problem. Problem-solving skills empower your child and show them that they are in control of their emotions, not the other way around.

Challenges Highly Sensitive Children Face

Highly sensitive children face several challenges when they are learning to regulate their emotions. Keep in mind that you are teaching a child who is used to expressing themselves through crying, screaming, or throwing tantrums to control their feelings and remain calm even during intense situations.

Understand that when your child gets overwhelmed, they can't control their reactions because they often can't separate themselves from their emotions. So, when you tell them that these feelings don't define them and they have control over them, they may not fully understand you. Even when you apply these methods, they won't develop emotional intelligence right away. This will take time, and there will be moments when they go back to their old ways. For instance, one day, they will be upset and calmly tell you how they feel, and the next day they may throw tantrums.

Be patient with your child and understand they won't learn these techniques right away. They will experience ups and down, but in time, you will begin to see progress.

Offering Guidance

Parents should guide and support their children in developing effective emotional regulation skills.

Reward Their Behavior

Children understand the concepts of punishment and rewards. Each time your child practices emotional regulation, reward their behavior by making their favorite meal or buying them a small gift. This will encourage them to keep going and express themselves in a healthy way.

Allow Them to Express Their Emotions

Seeing that your child will go back and forth before learning to regulate their feelings, you should expect intense behavior now and then. Create a room or a small space at home where your child can safely express these feelings. When they can let it all out, they will feel in control.

Be Prepared for Triggering Situations

You have probably noticed there are certain situations that overwhelm your child or trigger their angry behavior. In some of these situations, there is nothing you can do, like when other kids at school don't let your child play with them. You can't always prevent every triggering incident, but you can have a plan whenever your child is exposed to one. Talk to your child and find out why these situations often get an intense reaction from them.

Remain Consistent

Remain consistent when teaching emotional regulation to your child. For instance, you can't make them feel accepted one day and then dismiss their feelings the next. This will confuse your child. Apply each method without wavering if you want to see real results.

Emotional intelligence is an essential skill for highly sensitive children. Your child feels lost and confused by their overwhelming feelings, and they don't know how to manage them. Emotional intelligence teaches them to separate themselves from their emotions and to learn healthy ways to express themselves.

3

CREATING A SUPPORTIVE HOME ENVIRONMENT

Highly-sensitive children require a controlled environment that supports their well-being and keeps unwanted triggers at bay. Creating and maintaining a supportive home environment is crucial as your unique child is hypersensitive to external stimuli. The calm and serene environment you'll provide them at home will support them in their journey of improved mental, physical, and emotional well-being, letting them navigate their daily lives with confidence.

Structure and consistency are two pillars of creating an encouraging home environment. Structuring adequate routines and frameworks which promote a sense of security for the children and sticking to these routines is crucial to achieving the best outcomes. Knowing what to expect and when can alleviate anxiety and allow them to manage their emotions better. By implementing consistent schedules for meals, sleep, and activities, parents can help create a sense of order that supports their child's overall well-being.

Setting aside a quiet and peaceful space within the home is also essential for highly sensitive children. This designated area will become a retreat where they can find solace and decompress when they feel overwhelmed by external stimuli. The space you create should be able to ward off unwanted sensory inputs, let the child recharge, be in solace, and regain their emotional balance. The area you create for your highly sensitive child can be anywhere from a quiet and comfy corner of a room to a fully dedicated space where they can retreat and indulge in activities that provide them peace of mind.

Continue providing emotional support while acknowledging the triggers and reassuring your little angel that being hypersensitive to certain external stimuli is a naturally acquired characteristic and can be controlled and regulated. Furthermore, ensure your child does not see their sensitivity as a weakness. Letting your child understand there's nothing wrong in experiencing these triggers, acknowledging the issue, and showing support give your child the determination and courage to better cope with the challenges they face.

Besides creating a calm environment for your child, encourage open communication, letting them speak their heart out, and not judging them for their feelings and opinions. Staying empathetic and listening actively will assure your child that they are valued and understood. As you foster better communication, assist them in developing relevant skills and strategies to regulate their emotions and be communicative to let your child navigate the world around them hassle-free.

Why a Supportive Home Environment Is Necessary

It's paramount to create a nurturing home environment to cater to your child's unique needs. Understanding the specific triggers makes it easier to provide an environment tailored to their needs. Let's dig deep into the necessity of creating a supportive home environment.

Acknowledging Sensitivities

Children highly sensitive to external stimuli need an environment that accommodates their sensitivities and support from parents and caregivers to acknowledge their issues. Their sensitivities to stimuli vary. Knowing the effect and extent of the hypersensitivity caused by an external stimulus will let you create an environment that will alleviate unnecessary stressors, creating a sense of calm. For example, if your child is hypersensitive to bright lights and loud noises, limiting their exposure will let your child calm down their nerves.

Building Emotional Resilience

Furthermore, creating this environment gives your child a way to express their emotions. Actively listening to your child and showing empathy will give your child the confidence to share their triggers and reduce the impact these triggers might have on their emotional and mental well-being. Providing a support mechanism that gives them reassurance in times of distress will make them emotionally secure and boost their self-confidence. This supportive approach cultivates a secure attachment between parent and child, laying the foundation for healthy emotional development.

Providing a Personal Space

Your highly sensitive child needs a place to spend alone time and away from potential triggers. The space you create will serve as a place of retreat when they feel overwhelmed by any external stimuli and let them recharge. Do encourage open dialogue and keep it supportive to express their feelings, concerns, and potential fears. Over time, your child will register it as a way of effective communication, fostering a bond of trust and understanding.

Lastly, the overall effects of the supportive environment will minimize stress and lay a foundation for empowering your child to navigate the world with confidence.

Strategies to Minimize Overstimulation

Make It Comfy

The home environment you create should include a designated space they can use as a place of retreat when in distress. Your aim is to keep triggers at bay, preventing excess noise, bright lights, and related stimuli from affecting your child. When creating the space, ensure you provide comfy seating using soft pillows, blankets, and sensory toys, which can keep your child from diverting their attention, and relaxed.

Use Soft Lighting

Children with increased sensitivities can also be affected by bright or fluorescent lighting. If possible, pick a space that gets natural light. However, if the natural light seems too bright, opt for soft and diffused lighting to create a soothing atmosphere. You can also use lamps with soft light and place them in different areas for coverage. When picking a light source, always choose warm-colored bulbs and consider using a dimmer to further fine-tune the brightness that suits your child.

Reduce Background Noise

While you can always shut windows and close doors when the triggering noises are coming from the neighborhood, understanding the noises produced within the household and controlling them is also crucial. Consider evaluating the noise levels inside the home, which could be a potential trigger. Lower the volume of electronic devices like television or any other entertainment gadget when necessary. Nevertheless, if it's not possible in the family environment, it's better to intervene by giving your child soft earplugs or noise-canceling headphones to reduce the external stimuli they receive.

Establish Predictable Routines

Children with sensitivities to external stimuli need to follow a predictable and consistent routine. Provide your child guidance on setting a daily routine and following it to reduce uncertainty. They will feel more confident with every milestone they achieve through the set routine. Allocate time for meals, play activities, and breaks throughout the day so they don't feel overwhelmed. Likewise, maintain a consistent bedtime routine where you can read them a storybook or spend some time showering your child with pure love and affection. Your child knowing what to expect, provides a sense of security, lowers anxiety, and keeps over-stimulating triggers at bay.

Organize the Space

Cluttered environments or disorganized spaces are potential stimuli that can create a sensory overload in hypersensitive children. Keeping the indoor space organized and tidy minimizes visual distractions. You can start by decluttering the space and removing objects, pieces of furniture, and any other item which doesn't belong. Use storage boxes, shelves, or containers to sort items and keep them organized. Reducing the visual clutter by organizing items and removing unwanted items reduces the chances of overstimulation.

Provide Sensory-Friendly Toys

When playing, provide sensory-friendly toys which can improve your child's control over their senses. Experiencing different materials, textures, and sounds produced by these sensory-friendly toys can train your child's brain to establish control over how they react to a sensation. These toys include stress balls, textured sensory bags, sensory bins, and weighted blankets which can significantly reduce stress and increase focus.

Create Visual Boundaries

Highly sensitive children often find solace in spaces created for them to relax and feel safe from unwanted triggers and stimuli. Defining the area as a personal space for your child will provide a sense of ownership. They will understand that whenever some triggers are creating too much stimulation, going to their personal space and relaxing will eventually calm them down. You can create visual boundaries by using household objects like room dividers, floor mats, carpets, or curtains. This visual boundary will give your child a sense of security and serenity, which is truly effective in regulating unwanted stimuli.

Offer Retreat Time

Keep track of when your child becomes too stimulated and ensure they always have an opportunity to relax and retreat, letting their senses simmer down. Soothing music, relaxation techniques, drawing, and reading are several activities that can induce a sense of calmness and better regulate their sensory experiences.

Practice Mindfulness Exercises

Teaching your child mindfulness and breathing exercises appropriate for their age can also reduce overstimulation. Deep breathing exercises and techniques like guided imagery can help your child stay relaxed, preventing them from getting over-whelmed.

Involve the Child

When designing a sensory-friendly space for your child, don't forget to get your child on board. Ask them about the colors they like or make arrangements the way they seem is feasible. You'll be developing a sense of ownership by taking their opinion and creating an environment that appeals to them.

Benefits of Establishing a Routine

Sense of Security

When you establish a routine, it induces a sense of security for your child. Following a schedule lets them understand what comes next, reducing uncertainty and curiosity linked with the event. The safer they feel, the more their emotional well-being will improve.

Reduces Overstimulation

By following a routine, your child will know what's coming and prepare themselves to meet the next activity well prepared. Knowing their routine aids in better managing their energy levels and prepares them for the transition from one task to another. Setting clear boundaries and a routine provides structure and a sense of order. The confidence gained from accomplishing daily tasks can also prevent your child from becoming overwhelmed by over-the-top sensory inputs or unexpected challenges.

Fosters Emotional Regulation

Predictable routines and clear boundaries provide highly sensitive children with a framework for emotional regulation. Consistent daily routines offer opportunities for regular breaks, rest, and self-care, allowing them to recharge and process their experiences. Clear boundaries also help them understand their own limits and communicate their needs effectively.

Enhances Communication

Open communication and collaboration among family members create an atmosphere of understanding and empathy. It encourages an atmosphere where open discussions about your child's sensitivities, needs, and any challenges they may be facing can be discussed frankly and sincerely. They can actively communicate and talk about their issues when following the routine. These insights can be used to further fine-tune the routine, making it more effective.

Development of Coping Skills

The daily routine you set for your child will improve their coping skills. When doing everyday tasks, they develop an understanding of tackling tasks. They will become more open and communicate any issues they are facing. This collaborative approach of discussing the tasks and providing guidance will let your child develop resilience and coping mechanisms.

Establishing predictable routines, promoting communication, setting clear boundaries, and providing unprecedented support to your child will create a supportive home environment that will surely make an impact.

Tips to Maintain the Routine

Minimizing Overstimulation

To keep your child following a routine, it's crucial to keep over-stimulating factors at bay. The home environment should be serene and peaceful, with minimal noise and lights. The areas where they engage in daily activities should be set for them, ensuring no external stimulus triggers are present. However, if the stimulus cannot be addressed, use interventions like earplugs for minimal exposure. The focus here is to reduce any form of overstimulation your child might face.

Teaching Time Management

Your highly sensitive child can also become overwhelmed when they have to perform a number of tasks in a short period. Teaching your child to deal with these situations early on can improve their time management skills, ensuring the routine is followed adequately. It won't be an issue for your child to follow the routine, as it should be crafted specifically to let them enjoy and learn from it. If your kid goes to school, work on supervising them while they manage their school work and other tasks due today. You can also inspire them to manage their routine by sharing your work routine and showing them how you manage time.

Establishing Predictable Routines

Always set a routine that your child enjoys and keep it predictable, so they know what's coming next. Always set times for specific tasks and include breaks in between to provide an energy boost. Most importantly, please remember to establish a sleep routine which is a natural way to reduce overstimulation, reduce stress build-up, and depression, so your child can perform in life with maximum efficiency. Help your child to prepare for transitions or changes with warnings and explanations in advance. This allows them to mentally prepare for shifts in activities or environments.

Setting Boundaries

Setting clear boundaries is crucial for highly sensitive children. Clearly communicate and reinforce boundaries regarding personal space, physical contact, and social interactions. Teach your child to identify and express their boundaries to others in a respectful manner. This gives them the courage to ask for what they want. Creating visual cues or signs, such as a "do not disturb" sign, can indicate when your child needs space or quiet time. It's important to respect your child's need for alone time and privacy, allowing them to have personal space where they feel safe and comfortable.

Promoting Self-Care

Encouraging self-care practices is essential for the well-being of highly sensitive children. Encourage your child to engage in activities that promote relaxation and self-soothing, such as reading, drawing, or listening to calming music. Teach them deep breathing exercises or mindfulness techniques to manage stress and anxiety effectively. Help your child identify and express their emotions, and guide them on healthy ways to cope. This may include journaling, talking to a trusted adult, or physical activities that help release tension. Encourage self-care practices such as getting enough sleep, eating nutritious meals, and getting regular physical activity that promotes their overall well-being.

Supporting Emotional Regulation

Supporting your highly sensitive child in developing emotional regulation skills is vital. Model and teach effective ways to manage emotions, such as using "I" statements to express feelings and needs clearly. Encourage open communication within the family, providing a safe space for your child to express their feelings without judgment. Active listening and validation of their emotions create an atmosphere of understanding and empathy. Help your child develop problem-solving skills to address challenging situations, teaching them how to identify alternatives, evaluate consequences, and make decisions. Supporting their emotional regulation journey involves providing guidance, patience, and positive reinforcement as they learn to navigate their emotions in a healthy way.

Remember, every child is unique, and observing and understanding your highly sensitive child's specific needs is crucial. These tips are general guidelines, but feel free to adapt them to suit your child's individual preferences and sensitivities. By implementing these strategies, parents can create a supportive environment that promotes well-being, self-regulation, and a healthy sense of self for their highly sensitive children.

4

EFFECTIVE COMMUNICATION STRATEGIES

Have you ever found yourself struggling to communicate with a highly sensitive child? It can often feel like walking through a minefield, unsure of how your words and actions will be received. Let's set the scene: you ask your child to clean up their toys, but instead of a compliant response, they burst into tears. Or maybe you make an innocent comment about the color of their shirt, only for it to be taken as a personal insult. These scenarios may seem trivial to some, but for parents of highly sensitive children, they are a daily reality. In this chapter, you'll get to understand the unique challenges of communicating with sensitive children. It will also provide effective strategies for fostering better communication and understanding within your family dynamic. So, let's get started!

Why Communication Is Challenging When Dealing with a Highly Sensitive Child

If you are a parent or caregiver of a highly sensitive child, you may have noticed that they struggle in social situations.

Processing verbal and non-verbal communication does not come easily to them because they over-process everything. Here are some more reasons why communication can be challenging for highly sensitive children:

1. Overwhelmed by Emotions: One of the biggest challenges that highly sensitive children face is being overwhelmed by their emotions. Since they experience emotions more intensely than others, they often find it difficult to express their feelings in an appropriate manner. For instance, a highly sensitive child may become very upset or overwhelmed when someone yells, even if it is not directed at them. This can make it difficult for them to communicate with others, as they may shut down or become defensive.

2. Difficulty Processing Information: Highly sensitive children also often struggle with processing information. They may become overwhelmed by too much input, making it difficult for them to hear what someone is saying or to understand instructions. They may also have trouble filtering out distractions and may get distracted by background noise or other environmental factors, making it hard for them to focus on what is being said.

3. Misunderstandings Due to Non-Verbal Cues: Highly sensitive children may also have difficulty interpreting non-verbal cues, including facial expressions, tone of voice, and body language. This lack of understanding can lead to misunderstandings and potential emotional meltdowns when messages are misinterpreted.

4. Fear of Rejection: Highly sensitive children are often very aware of the emotions of those around them and may be afraid of saying or doing something that will lead to rejection or judgment. They may be hesitant to express themselves openly, which can make it difficult for them to communicate their needs or desires effectively.

5. Difficulty in Social Situations: Highly sensitive children also face difficulties in social situations. They may become easily overwhelmed in group settings or have trouble knowing how to act in situations where there are many different social cues and expectations competing for their attention simultaneously.

6. Sensitivity to Criticism: Finally, highly sensitive children may have difficulty processing criticism or feedback. They may take criticism more personally than others or become overwhelmed by negative feedback, making it difficult for them to learn from their mistakes or grow.

Tips and Strategies for Enhancing Communication with Your Child

As parents, creating a secure and supportive environment goes a long way toward facilitating communication with your child. With this in mind, here are some practical tips and strategies for parents to encourage communication with their highly sensitive children:

1. Listen Actively and Empathetically

Active listening is all about concentrating focus on listening to your child, removing all distractions and turning off all electronics. Actively listening also involves acknowledging and reflecting on what your child is saying.

For example, if your child tells you that they are feeling sad because they were not invited to a friend's party, you can acknowledge their feelings by saying, "I can understand why you are feeling sad. It is hard not to be included in something that you would like to be a part of." This response validates your child's emotions and helps them feel heard.

Empathy is a crucial component of active listening and involves putting yourself in your child's shoes to understand how they feel. It is the ability to recognize and share the feelings of another and respond with a compassionate and supportive mindset. Empathy can help you understand why your child is feeling a certain way and offer support.

Consider another scenario: Your child comes to you upset because they received a low grade on their math test. As an empathetic listener, you can respond by saying, "I can imagine how frustrating it is to receive a low grade on a test. How can I help you study and prepare for the next math test?"

Empathy demonstrates that you are not dismissing your child's emotions but are taking them seriously and trying to help in any way possible. It also shows that you understand your child's point of view and are trying to help them navigate challenging situations.

2. Give Them Space and Time to Decompress

Another effective strategy to enhance communication with your highly sensitive child is to give them space and time to decompress. As an empathetic and caring parent, you may be tempted to constantly check in with your child, but it is important to recognize that they need breaks from social interactions and external stimuli to recharge.

For example, if your child comes home from school feeling emotionally drained, you can let them know that it is okay to take some time to themselves. Encourage them to find a quiet spot, such as their bedroom or a cozy nook in the house, where they can relax and recharge. Providing a safe and comfortable space for your child to retreat to shows that you understand and respect their needs. This action also acts as a way to support their processing of emotions and helps them to discover their own ways of getting into a stable state once again.

During this time, your child can do things that help them relax and release tension, such as reading a book, practicing deep breathing exercises, or listening to calming music. By doing this, your child is able to develop mindfulness, which is an effective strategy for managing intense emotions; they become mindful of their emotional states and are better equipped to handle them.

Once your child has had some time to decompress and recharge, you can resume communication with them calmly and supportively. Not bombarding them with questions or demands for immediate communication and letting them come to you could considerably ease the situation. This allows your child to process their emotions and thoughts at their own pace before engaging in any conversation.

3. Help Them Label Their Emotions

One effective strategy to enhance communication with your highly sensitive child is to create a safe space where they can label and understand their emotions. This means helping them to identify and name their feelings and to understand what is causing them to feel that way. By doing this, you will be providing them with the tools and language they need to communicate their emotions effectively and to seek support when they need it.

You can create a "feelings chart" with pictures or emoji's that represent different emotions and encourage your child to point to the one that best describes how they are feeling. This can be especially helpful for younger children who may not have the vocabulary to label their emotions.

You can also help your child understand the connection between their feelings and behavior. For example, if your child is acting out or throwing a tantrum, talk to them about how their emotions are affecting their behavior, and help them come up with strategies to regulate their emotions in a more positive way.

4. Avoid Negative Criticism and Promote Positive Reinforcement

To begin, avoid negative criticism and instead offer constructive feedback. The first step in doing so is to acknowledge and validate your child's feelings. For example, if your child is struggling with a particularly challenging task, such as completing a difficult math problem, you might start by acknowledging their frustration and offering words of encouragement. You might say, "I know this is really tough, but I believe in you. You've got this."

Positive reinforcement also includes highlighting your child's strengths and accomplishments. Whether it is a successful test score, a completed project, or a new skill they have learned, taking the time to recognize and acknowledge your child's accomplishments can build their confidence and self-esteem. For instance, you might say, "I'm so proud of how hard you worked on that project. You really put in a lot of effort, and it shows."

Engaging your child in positive, encouraging conversations about their interests and passions may also be helpful. By encouraging your child to explore and pursue activities they enjoy, you can help them build self-confidence and develop a sense of purpose and direction.

5. Practice and Promote Mindfulness

Parenting a highly sensitive child can be frustrating and tiresome. There is always a chance of accumulating residual anger, and if you are not able to release your mental tension, take it out on your child.

This is why practicing and promoting mindfulness with your child can help you both stay calm, centered, and focused during conversations.

One example of how you might use mindfulness while communicating with your child is during a moment of conflict or tension. In this situation, take a moment to pause, slow down your breathing, and focus on the present moment. Try to observe your thoughts and feelings without reacting to them. This mindful approach will help you to respond to your child's emotional state with empathy and understanding rather than with frustration or anger.

Another mindfulness technique you might use is visualization. This involves using your imagination to create a mental image of a peaceful or calming scene. For example, you might envision a quiet beach with gentle waves lapping at the shore or a peaceful meadow with a warm breeze blowing through the grass. This visual imagery can help you and your child to relax and feel more centered during stressful or overwhelming situations.

Deep breathing exercises are also an effective way to reduce tension and anxiety. When you or your child feel stressed or overwhelmed, take a moment to focus on your breath. Inhale deeply through your nose, hold your breath for a few seconds, and then exhale slowly through your mouth. Repeat this process several times until you feel more calm and relaxed.

6. Model Appropriate Behavior

Children are astute observers and tend to imitate their parent's behavior, especially during their formative years. As a parent, it's essential to be mindful of your actions and words in your child's presence and act as a role model for them. Your behavior impacts your child's emotional and social development, so setting a positive example for them is crucial.

A highly sensitive child usually has difficulties dealing with their emotions, and they look up to you for guidance and support. By modeling appropriate behavior, you show your child the tools they need to manage their emotions and cope with difficult situations. This means using positive language, showing empathy towards others, and practicing self-care. Here are a few examples of how you can model appropriate behavior for your child:

1. Use positive language: It's essential to use positive language when communicating with your child to encourage them to do the same. Avoid being negative; it can be hurtful and discouraging. For instance, instead of saying, "You're not good enough," you can say, "I believe in you, and I know you can do this."

2. Show empathy towards others: Highly sensitive children are often empathetic and compassionate towards others. As a parent, you can model this behavior by showing empathy towards others. Talk to your child about other people's feelings and perspectives and encourage them to be kind and understanding.

3. Practice self-care: Self-care is crucial for your child's emotional and mental well-being. If they see you taking care of yourself, they'll be more likely to follow suit. Take some time out for yourself to exercise, meditate, or engage in any activity that helps you relax and rejuvenate.

7. Work on Creating Routines

Highly sensitive children struggle to adapt to new environments or activities without proper preparation. A predictable routine gives them a sense of control and structure, alleviating some of their anxiety and making them feel more comfortable.

To create a predictable routine, start by establishing a consistent daily schedule. This could include set times for waking up, meals, schoolwork, playtime, and bedtime. Try to stick to this schedule as closely as possible, even on weekends and holidays. This will help your child anticipate what's coming next and feel more in control of their day.

It's also helpful to provide your child with a visual schedule, such as a chart or calendar. This helps them see what activities they will be doing throughout the day and feel more prepared for what's ahead. Use pictures or symbols to represent each activity, especially for younger children who cannot read yet.

For example, you could create a chart with pictures of breakfast, getting dressed, brushing teeth, going to school, coming home, snack time, playtime, dinner, and bedtime. Hang this chart in a prominent place, such as on the refrigerator or in your child's bedroom. This way, your child can refer to it throughout the day and stay on track with their routine.

Another way to create a predictable routine is to establish rituals or traditions around certain activities. For example, you could have a special song you sing when it's time to clean up toys or a specific bedtime routine that includes reading a story and saying goodnight to each stuffed animal. These rituals can help your child feel more connected to the activity and make it feel less overwhelming.

It's critical to be flexible with your routine, too. Sometimes unexpected things happen, and you may need to adapt your schedule to accommodate them. If this happens, try to prepare your child as much as possible for the change. Let them know what's happening, why it's happening, and what they can expect. This will help them feel more in control of the situation and reduce their anxiety.

Conflict Resolution Strategies for Parents

It can be challenging to navigate conflicts with your highly sensitive child. But, the sensitive nature of your kid makes it necessary to approach conflict with care and understanding. Here are five conflict resolution strategies that you can use to foster understanding and validate your highly sensitive child's feelings.

1. Acknowledge Your Child's Feelings

The first step is to acknowledge their feelings. By acknowledging their feelings, you validate their experience and let them know you understand. For example, if your child is upset because they feel like you aren't listening to them, you can say, "I hear that you're feeling unheard, and that must be frustrating for you."

2. Use Empathy

Empathy is key to effective conflict resolution. By putting yourself in your child's shoes and seeing things from their perspective, you can better understand their feelings and needs. For example, if your child is upset because they are being teased at school, you can say, "I can understand how that would be hurtful for you. It's tough to be teased, and it's okay to feel upset about it."

3. Collaborate on Solutions

Collaborating with your child on solutions to conflicts can help them feel like their voice is heard and that their opinions matter. By involving them in the process, you are showing them that you respect their input. For example, if your child is upset because they don't like their after-school program, you can say, "Let's brainstorm some other after-school activities that you think you would enjoy. Maybe we can come up with something together."

4. Provide Reassurance

Children may worry about the impact of conflicts on their relationships with others. Providing reassurance can help alleviate those fears and make them feel safe and loved. For example, if your child is upset because they made a mistake that upset a friend, you can say, "Everyone makes mistakes. You're still a great friend, and I know you'll work to make things right."

5. Encourage Self-Expression

Highly sensitive children may struggle with expressing their feelings and needs, which could lead to conflict. Encouraging self-expression can help them feel more comfortable sharing their thoughts and feelings. For example, if your child is upset because they don't want to go to a family event, you can say, "It's okay to feel nervous about going to the event. Can you tell me more about what's making you feel that way?"

5

MANAGING OVERWHELM AND ANXIETY

Anxiety is a normal challenge for children. Suppose you have a child suffering from deep emotional responsiveness or sensory processing disorder (SPD). In that case, you may have seen first-hand how such a disorder can lead to or amplify anxiety in your child. Sensory disorders can be unbearable for a child, regardless of the degree of their effect.

For example, for a child prone to sensory input, a normal voice tone might sound excruciatingly loud to that child. Hence, kids prone to sensory input may naturally avoid situations where they will be offended easily.

The recurring thought of encountering situations that may affect a child's sensory input can cause such a child to worry. When a child worries this much, anxiety becomes the normal response of the day. Parents are in a better position to assist their children in overcoming anxiety and building healthy habits, attitudes, and responsiveness.

This chapter is a complete guide to strategies for managing and reducing overwhelming feelings and anxiety in your child. It also entails relaxation techniques and mindfulness practices for managing stress and anxiety. You will also be getting tips on how you can help your child deal with their anxiety and the importance of parental support in assisting children in the development of healthy coping mechanisms.

Strategies for Effectively Managing and Reducing Overwhelm and Anxiety

It is normal to be disturbed when your child experiences anxiety. However, you may employ methods to minimize your child's anxiety, especially if they are overwhelmed due to their immaturity and lack of exposure to the outside world. As your child navigates life's challenges and stressful periods, supporting them in managing and reducing their anxiety is vital. Below are some strategies for managing and reducing your child's anxiety and overwhelming feelings.

- **Figure Out the Triggers**

Identifying triggers is the first helpful step in managing your child's anxiety. As parents or caregivers, you must be aware of and identify the things or situations that cause your child to become extremely anxious. Once you have identified these triggers, the other strategies will be easier to execute.

- **Practice Deep Breathing**

Deep breathing is a technique that enables one to think, refocus, and relax. It helps decrease stress, heart and breathing rates, and muscle tension. It also helps boost the oxygen level in the blood-stream. To achieve deep breathing, do the following:

1. Teach your children to lay their hands on their belly and chest. Let them know that the objective of this instruction is to breathe deeply with their bellies, which will cause the hand placed on their tummy to move up and down as they breathe in and breathe out air. They will know they are breathing with their chest more as the hand on the chest moves more. Motivate them to breathe more using their bellies.

2. Teach them to breathe slowly through their nose, hold out for some time, and then let it out through their mouth. Go over this exercise as many times as possible. You can spice up this exercise by pretending to blow out birthday cakes or smell a flower.

- **Validate and Sympathize**

It is vital that your children are heard and that their thoughts, experiences, and emotions, which matter most to them, are validated and acknowledged. Visualize what it would be like to experience what they are feeling and be more understanding of their feelings in the future since it matters to them.

- **Practice Role-plays**

Some specific events cause children to feel overwhelmed or anxious. Therefore, practice role-playing by playing out such events to prepare them for how to act in such situations. For instance, you may act out situations such as asking a friend over, purchasing a movie ticket, asking a teacher for assistance, or ordering at a restaurant.

- **Question Unhelpful Thinking**

Give your children room to discuss their thoughts with you, especially those unhelpful ones that cause stress. Such thoughts could be, "I am not good enough," or "I am not going to ace my math test and might fail the class." You can work with your children to bring about more reasonable and accommodating thoughts once you are aware of the thoughts they are telling themselves. Help them see their situation differently by asking questions. This would enable them to unsubscribe from unhelpful thought patterns. Ask questions like, "What made you feel you were not good enough?" "Have you ever failed to ace your math test before?" and "In the past, what were the things you did to ace a test? Why can't you do those things now?"

Questions like these enable your children to ponder the situation and draw conclusions from their thoughts. Telling children they will not fail, whether as a parent, peer, or teacher, would do little compared to them realizing it for themselves. As you succeed in questioning the unhelpful thoughts in your children, motivate them to begin to build more attainable, friendly thoughts like, "Though I may fail, I have prepared myself for the math test and will perform the best." or "My failing the test does not mean that I am going to fail the class." Lofty thoughts like "I will pass and be amazing" are unrealistic and unnecessary and do not help children.

Relaxation Techniques to Promote Emotional Regulation and Reduce Stress

Relaxation techniques are a major way to manage stress and boost emotional regulation. Relaxation is more than just enjoying a hobby or peace of mind. It also entails the reduction of stress's effect on the mind and body of your child. Your child can handle everyday stress at home or school through relaxation techniques. These relaxation techniques can also assist in managing long-term stress or stress-connected health challenges such as sensory processing disorder. The following are some relaxation techniques for reducing stress and promoting emotional regulation.

- ## Deep Breathing

Deep breathing is a technique where your child takes long, slow, deep belly breaths. As the child breathes, their mind is slowly released from distracting sensations and thoughts. Children with eating disorders or those prone to severe anxiety can benefit from the deep breathing technique since it helps their bodies focus positively. However, it is a technique unsuitable for children with health challenges associated with difficulty in breathing, such as heart defects, asthma, etc.

- ## Guided Imagery or Visualization

In this technique, teach your child to create calming scenes, experiences, or places in their mind to enable them to focus and relax. Additionally, search online for free recordings and apps depicting calming scenes that benefit your child. Visualization can help children sustain a positive version of themselves. However, this technique might be challenging for those with intrusive thoughts, as it would be difficult for them to create mental images.

- ## Body Scan

The body scan combines deep breathing techniques and gradual muscle relaxation. At the end of a few minutes of deep belly breathing, fix your child's attention on one part of their body at a time to mentally let go of any physical tension they might be feeling. That spot. Body scan techniques enable children to develop consciousness of the mind and body relationship.

This method may not be as accommodating for kids who have had surgery that left a scar on their body.

- **Mindfulness Meditation**

This technique requires that your child comfortably sit down, concentrate on their breathing, and direct their mind's attention to present happenings without considering past or future events. This aspect of meditation has gained popularity over the years. According to research, mindfulness meditation is vital for kids with pain, anxiety, and depression.

- **Repetitive Prayer**

Repetitive prayer involves instructing your child to silently say a short prayer or phrase repeatedly alongside the practice of deep breathing. If you are a spiritual or religious enthusiast, you or your child can find meaning in this technique.

- **Tai chi, Yoga, and Qigong**

These three age-old arts combine deep breathing with a couple of postures. The physical part of these practices enables your child to be mentally focused, which helps them fight racing thoughts. It also improves their balance and flexibility. Experts suggest trying several techniques and seeing which one works best for your child instead of choosing one.

However, these techniques become challenging if they have a disabling condition or certain health problems that might prevent them. Consult with your doctor before you let your child undergo these techniques.

- **Manage Their Social Media Time**

Social media sites are good interactive platforms. At the same time, they can become stressful based on the long hours your child spends with them and the things they might see. These long hours could be better spent visiting friends and enjoying their company. Your child could even spend that time reading a great book or enjoying the weather outside. One other thing parents or caregivers fail to realize is that when you let children use social media at night, it worsens their sleep condition by making them have fewer hours of sound sleep due to the increased stress they would have accumulated at that time.

Mindfulness Practices and Grounding Exercises for Managing Anxiety

Children may experience anxiety to a degree where they go over the edge and cannot control their feelings. When anxiety is not properly managed, and this dangerous point is reached, your child might turn to unhealthy and damaging activities to try to cope. To avoid such mental health damage, grounding and mindfulness practices are the tools you're going to need to help your child deal with anxiety. They restore attention to your child's physical experience and stop them from becoming prisoners of their racing, intrusive thoughts.

Here are some grounding exercises and mindfulness practices to manage anxiety.

- **Holding Objects**

You can ground your children's anxiety by immersing their focus deeply on an object and how it feels. Consider these steps for this process:

1. Choose any object that fits your hand well. This object could be a smooth stone, light paper, or an object with great texture.

2. Instruct them to hold the object in the palm of their hand, focusing their attention on how it feels and looks.

3. Encourage them to consider the object's colors, sparkling, light-reflecting, or shadow-emitting nature.

4. Guide them to meditate on the object's dry, coarse, smooth, soft, or rippled texture.

5. Ask them questions such as, "Is the object unevenly weighted and heavy or balanced and feels light?"

This exercise aims to get your children's attention off whatever is bothering them, keep them in the present, and ground them in the object.

The Five Senses

Using your child's five senses is a great way to take their focus off anxiety triggers and redirect them to their present environment.

To engage your child's five senses, follow the guidelines provided:

1. Instruct your child to sit down with closed eyes and take a few long, deep breaths in through the nostrils and out through the mouth. Bring their focus back to each breath as they reach a state of calm.

2. Next, instruct them to open their eyes and ask the following questions, either to themselves or out loud:

- What can I taste?
- What can I hear?
- What can I smell?
- What can I see?
- What can I feel?

3. Get them to stay in the moment while these questions are being asked, focusing their attention on each of their senses

4. When it is time to end the exercise, they should take a few deep breaths.

- **Three Minutes Breathing Space Meditation**

Mindful breathing and grounding go hand in hand. Breathing exercises are a powerful, effective, and rapid technique to bring your child's mind and body back to the present and let them regain equilibrium.

Have your child sit straight and comfortable with their eyes shut, directing their minds to their internal experience. Use these steps as a guideline for mindful breathing.

Step One

Encourage them to go over their experience by pondering the following:

1. The thoughts that run through their minds. Help them focus on their thoughts and see them as in pictures.

2. What are they feeling at the moment? Help them recognize their emotions without trying to interfere with the emotion.

3. What sensations in the body are they feeling right now? Help them to be conscious of any discomfort or tightness in their mind without trying to influence such sensations.

Step Two

Bring your findings in and concentrate.

1. Encourage your child to imagine a spotlight following the small sensations they feel accompanying each breath.

2. Encourage your child to get closer to the sensation of the breath in their belly and notice it contracting and expanding. Gradually place your hand on their stomach if that helps you.

3. Encourage them to be focused

Step Three

Widen your attention.

1. Encourage them to increase their consciousness of their breath and feel it throughout their whole body.

2. Allow them to breathe with awareness feeling any tension or discomfort, and let each breath move around any possible sensations.

3. Encourage them to learn and be able to express these sensations instead of trying to change them.

When finishing the exercise, they can take a few slow, deep breaths and open their eyes. Their focus now should be on their environment as they carry the calmness they feel into the rest of their day.

- **Ask Questions**

Anxiety has a way of making children feel detached, disconnected, and non-existent. Practicing mindfulness can redirect their focus to the here and now. Therefore, teach your child to always challenge every thought when they feel panicky and on edge.

Teach them to ask themselves certain questions and write the answers down, preferably in their journal, whenever they sense a feeling of anxiety. They should ask questions such as:

- How old am I?
- Where am I right now?
- Where do I live?
- Who do I live with?
- What season is it?
- What day and what month is it?

- **Grounding Chair**

Just by sitting still, your child can regain a sense of feeling grounded, which can be carried out anywhere. Help them be conscious of the person between them and their seat, the texture of the seating material, and their weight against the chair's surface.

They should apply pressure to the ground from one of their feet only when they feel ready. Encourage your child to visualize the heaviness leaving their mind and body going into the ground; as it leaves their body, tell them to feel the lightness in every part of their body.

Then, guide them to take a few light breaths and bring their attention back to the room when they are ready to end the exercise. After the exercise, ask them how they feel and whether they feel lighter, less burdened, and more in the moment.

- **Positive Coping Statements**

Parents or caregivers can construct a well-written coping statement that reflects their child's values and give it to them whenever they might feel as if they are losing touch with reality, feeling overwhelmed, or anxious. For instance:

My name is Y, named after XYZ. I am loved and wanted. Everything happening now is here to make me better, not bitter. It has not come to stay; this will pass away like other things before it. At the end of this episode, I will look back without any sense of fear or anxiety.

Encourage them to say such written statements over and over again till every word begins to make sense to them and they begin to see the temporary nature of the events come to pass.

Importance of Parental Support and Modeling in Assisting Their Child Develop Healthy Coping Mechanisms

Parental support and modeling can help children develop coping strategies that positively influence their mental health when experiencing a mental breakdown. Naturally, as the first teacher in a child's life, parents should model the right coping skills. Children are more likely to base their behaviors on how they relate to what they have learned from their parents. A study shows that adolescents who use avoidance coping mechanisms are more likely to use marijuana. This example is due to the absence of the right coping mechanisms during their childhood.

Conversely, children who learn healthy coping mechanisms early can manage mental and physical issues and enjoy some wonderful benefits later in life. Researchers also discovered that kids who learn how to control and manage their emotions at the tender age of five have a high percentage of college educations and steady jobs as adults. These children are less susceptible to substance abuse, mental health issues, and criminal activity.

Tips and Tricks on How Parents Can Help Their Children Manage Their Anxiety

When your kids experience an episode of anxiety, they may be overwhelmed, agitated, and worried, which could lead to a panic attack. The following tips and tricks are useful for moments like this to help your kids stay calm and safe.

- **Breathe Deeply and Slowly with Them**

You can count to five, breathe in together, and count to five again as you breathe out together. If the count is hard, make it shorter, but encourage your child to breathe.

- **Sit With Them While Offering Calm Physical Assurance**

Hold their hands and let them be in your presence. You may even offer to cuddle them to help calm them down.

- **Reassure Them That the Anxiety Will Pass**

Assure them that they will be okay. They may be soothed if you describe the anxiety as a wave in the ocean that comes and goes.

- **Use All Five Senses Together**

Refer to what your child can see, smell, touch, hear, and taste to help bring their focus back to the present moment.

- **Motivate Them to Do Something That Helps Them Feel Calmer**

Encourage any activity that helps to get your child into the present moment. Their comfort activities may include swimming, walking, visiting the cinema, or writing.

Managing overwhelm and anxiety in your child with the techniques above should no longer be a challenge. As with any technique, trick, or strategy, know that you and your child must practice it diligently. Be mindful that the result you see in your child is tied to their willingness to follow through on the techniques, mindful practices, and grounded exercises. Furthermore, ensure that you model the right coping mechanisms for your children. When all these are followed, your child's mental health will certainly improve.

6

BUILDING RESILIENCE

Not everyone in the world is going to be understanding of your highly sensitive child and tolerant of their little quirks and traits. Although you can do your best to support your child when they're young, you cannot always be with them wherever they go. They will most likely have to face difficulties in their lives and learn how to cope with them on their own. To do this, they have to be resilient in the face of challenges, whether it's difficult situations or problematic people. To help them become resilient and strong, you need to empower your child so they feel confident in their skin and not ashamed of who they are and what they feel. Being highly sensitive is not a mental disease and should not be treated as such. It is simply the way they are, so instead of walking on eggshells around them, validate their feelings and teach them how to deal with problems on their own.

Empower Your Highly Sensitive Child

The best way to empower your highly sensitive child is by acknowledging their sensitivity and giving them the necessary tools and techniques to deal with any issues they face. Here are some ways you can empower your HSC:

1. Name Their Feelings

Helping children identify and name their emotions can make a big difference to how they manage their emotional highs and lows. It's essential to teach children feeling words and demonstrate how to express those emotions appropriately. When children find it challenging to articulate their feelings and shut down, connecting the situation with the emotions they are experiencing removes the reason for a meltdown.

Using non-verbal methods can be helpful for younger kids who find it hard to talk about their feelings. Here's a simple idea you can try to grab some index cards and draw different facial expressions like happy, sad, or angry on them. Then, when you want to know how your children are feeling, just show them the cards and let them point to the one that matches their emotions best. Another option is to use sticky notes with checkboxes for easy responses like "yes," "no," and "maybe." This way, even if they don't feel like talking, they can still communicate by writing down their answers to direct questions. These small changes in how you communicate can make a big difference. They can help bridge the gap between feeling frustrated and having effective communication with your sensitive child.

2. Never Punish Feelings

Disciplining a crying child can lead to more tears or suppressed and unpredictable anger. When a child feels their emotions are not accepted, they begin to internalize them. However, repressed emotions are not easily controlled consciously and might manifest as "bad" behavior later on. For instance, if a child is upset about losing a toy and is scolded or punished for crying, they may learn to suppress their feelings, believing that showing emotions is unacceptable. Consequently, this child might grow up with difficulties expressing their emotions, leading to potential outbursts or emotional challenges in the future.

Punishing a child for crying does not foster positive traits like compassion, empathy, or confidence in them. For example, if a child is upset about a disappointing event at school and is punished for expressing their feelings openly, they will likely struggle to develop empathy for others who experience similar emotions. This lack of empathy could prevent them from forming strong, healthy relationships with their peers and inhibit their emotional growth.

3. Avoid dismissive statements

Avoid dismissive statements like "relax" or "let it go" when coaching a child's feelings. Instead, focus on empathetic and supportive phrases that encourage emotional expression and understanding. Here are some examples:

- "I can see that you're feeling sad/angry/frustrated. It's okay to feel that way, and I'm here to listen."
- "Tell me more about what's bothering you. Your feelings are valid, and I want to understand."
- "I'm sorry you're going through this. How can I help or support you right now?"
- "I know it can be tough, but remember, I love you no matter how you feel."
- "I'm not here to judge you; I just want to understand what you're experiencing."
- "Take your time to express yourself. I'm here to listen without interrupting or judging."

- "Your feelings are important, and I'm grateful you trust me enough to share them."
- "Let's find healthy ways to cope with these emotions. We can figure this out together."
- "You're not alone in feeling this way. We all have ups and downs, and it's okay to talk about them."

4. Have Empathetic Boundaries

Setting clear boundaries with understanding and compassion is essential when guiding a child's behavior. Being compassionate doesn't mean being permissive; rather, it involves acknowledging their feelings and needs while maintaining appropriate limits.

To elaborate on this, let's consider the example of a child asking for a new toy. Instead of simply saying, "No, you can't have it," a compassionate response would be, "I understand that you really want this toy, and I appreciate your excitement. However, right now, we have a budget for toys, and we need to prioritize other things. Let's see if we can find a compromise or plan for it in the future."

Similarly, when a child misbehaves, instead of only reprimanding them, an understanding approach could be, "I see that you're upset, but hitting your sister is not an acceptable way to express your feelings. Let's talk about what happened and find a better way for you to express your emotions."

Help Them Develop Coping Skills

Helping highly sensitive kids develop coping skills is essential to support their emotional well-being and help them navigate the challenges they may face in their everyday lives. Here are some strategies you can try:

1. Prepare for Everything

Sensitive kids function best when they are put in a predictable routine with familiar situations so that they know what's coming their way. For instance, consider the first day of school. If you throw them into this experience without any preparation, they will feel overwhelmed at every turn. On the other hand, if you introduce them to the idea of a classroom, take them to meet their teacher, and get familiarized with their surroundings first, they'll feel considerably more at ease. These kids often worry a lot about what others think of them, which can make them freeze in the moment. To help them out, you can work with them to come up with some cool responses they can use in different situations. Role-playing these scenarios can be a fun way to practice together. Team up with your kid and find ways to deal with stress in a healthy way. You can even create a little toolkit with ideas that work for them. It could be things like breathing exercises, tearing up paper, squishing play dough, stomping around, or pretending to be their favorite animals.

2. Create Boundaries and Safe Spaces

Sensitive children tend to absorb a lot from their surroundings and react strongly to them. To avoid unnecessary challenges, a little prevention goes a long way. For infants, it's helpful to keep their sleeping area as quiet as possible. As kids grow older, they'll need opportunities for downtime after they've been through busy and stimulating activities. Setting boundaries is crucial, enabling them to process their emotions safely. For instance, if they have hockey practice and a birthday party on one day, both of which involve a lot of emotional energy, it might be better to plan some downtime in between.

3. Practice Gentle Discipline

One of the remarkable traits of highly sensitive children is their keen awareness of hypocrisy and morality. They're quick to notice if a situation seems unfair or if someone fails to keep their promises. When it comes to discipline, approach it with care, as these children are already prone to self-criticism when they feel they've done something wrong. Gentle discipline is the way to go here. It means setting clear limits without judgment and ensuring that consequences are fair and aligned with your family rules and norms. The key is not to make it personal. Instead of saying, "You can't have iPad time because you're a bad kid," use a more positive approach like, "The iPad time can wait until you finish your homework ." The emotions of sensitive children run deep, and emotional memories stick with them more intensely. Especially harmful is shame, which can have a toxic impact on them.

4. Validate Their Feelings

Sensitive children often find themselves in situations where their emotional reactions are misunderstood or brushed off by parents and peers. One of the most valuable things you can do for these kids with big feelings is to validate them. Put yourself in their shoes and let them know you genuinely want to connect with them. Instead of trying to solve their problems right away, take the time to acknowledge and sit with their uncomfortable emotions. For example, rather than saying, "Why do you think nobody likes you?" you can say, "It must have been tough when Bobby didn't want to play with you today." By validating their feelings, you're helping them jumpstart the process of coping, calming down, and dealing with those emotions in a healthy way.

As your children grow older, maintaining an emotional connection with them remains vital. If they don't develop the necessary tools to handle their big feelings, there's a risk they might turn to less healthy coping strategies or behaviors. If you stay tuned into their emotions, you'll be better equipped to offer the support they need as their world becomes more complex. Most importantly, they'll know they can always turn to you for that extra support and understanding. Being there for them emotionally can make all the difference in helping them navigate life with confidence and resilience.

5. Teach Them to Be Confident

Many kids who are very sensitive find themselves facing challenges that require self-confidence. It could be making new friends or trying something new. They worry about feeling embarrassed and how others might react. To help them gain confidence, and feel comfortable being themselves, here are some effective tips you can try:

1. Sensitivity Is Normal

Many highly sensitive children (HSCs) notice their differences from other kids at a young age. This feeling might become more apparent when they're hesitant to try new things or feel scared in group situations at school. Ignoring this issue could negatively impact their attitude and beliefs about high sensitivity and damage their self-confidence.

To help your child, explain that high sensitivity is a trait found in around one in five people, meaning there are likely other highly sensitive kids among their friends and peers. Emphasize the positive attributes associated with this trait, allowing them to see themselves in a better light despite the challenges. This approach will enable them to gain more confidence in their inherent qualities, talents, and learning abilities in the long run.

2. Actively Listen

Pay attention when they share their thoughts and ideas. Let them know you're interested in what they have to say. It's tough for kids when they get interrupted or face constant criticism, so be patient and supportive. You don't have to agree with everything, but listen carefully and share your thoughts too. If they come up with something great, praise them! And if they have not-so-great ideas, don't shoot them down. Instead, explain why you might have a different view and help them see how they could improve. Having open and honest conversations with your little one will build their self-confidence over time.

3. Be a Role Model

Remember, you're your child's first teacher, and they're watching everything you do. Whether consciously or unconsciously, they'll try to model themselves after you. So, if you're a bit shy or easily intimidated, your highly sensitive child will pick up on it too. Don't worry; developing self-confidence doesn't happen overnight, but you can work on it at your own pace. In the meantime, try to appear self-confident, even if you don't feel it yet. Body language experts suggest some tricks used by confident people, like standing tall and making eye contact when talking to others. Your highly sensitive child will notice and probably start imitating your confident actions. It's like a little confidence ripple effect! So, lead by example, and together, you'll grow in confidence.

4. Teach Them about Self-Motivation

You can help your child develop confidence considerably by teaching them these three impactful phrases:

- **I can do it**

When your child says this, it enhances their belief in their skills and talents. Over time, this positive affirmation empowers them to believe in themselves, especially when faced with challenges.

- **I want to make an effort**

This phrase emphasizes the importance of self-motivation. Self-confidence requires drive and resilience even when confronted with difficulties or unpleasant situations.

- **I will give it a good try**

Beyond merely starting something, this statement encourages your child to give their best effort to achieve their desired outcomes. However, it's essential for them to understand that confidence doesn't guarantee success.

For highly sensitive children, handling mistakes and failures can be particularly challenging. They may tend to blame themselves, irrespective of the actual cause, leading to a negative impact on their self-confidence and self-esteem. As a supportive parent, explain to your child that failures are valuable opportunities for learning and growth. They should not be seen as definitive or permanent setbacks. While confidence grows with success, facing and overcoming failures can build resilience in children. Guide your highly sensitive child to adopt this mindset so their self-confidence remains intact even when they experience setbacks or don't achieve their goals. With your encouragement and understanding, they'll grow into more confident individuals, ready to face life's challenges with determination and self-assurance.

5. Visualization techniques

Visualization is a powerful technique that can help highly sensitive children build their confidence and face challenges with a positive mindset. As natural deep thinkers, this approach aligns perfectly with their abilities. Here's how you can use visualization to empower your child:

· **Prepare for upcoming events**: If your child has an important event, like a performance at school, encourage them to visualize success. Have them imagine the applause and smiles from the audience, as well as the compliments they might receive.

·**Focus on the positive**: Visualization directs their attention towards positive outcomes, which boosts their willingness and confidence to tackle the challenge head-on.

· **Reduce worries**: By concentrating on the positive aspects, they can keep worries and self-doubt at bay, helping them approach the situation with greater self-assurance.

Visualization is an easy-to-adopt and effective tool. It taps into their imagination and helps them see themselves achieving their goals. With this technique, your highly sensitive child can develop a can-do attitude and face various situations with renewed confidence.

6. Dissuade your child from engaging in self-criticism

Highly sensitive children tend to take mistakes and failures to heart, carrying the weight of wrong decisions even when they aren't entirely responsible. They tend to criticize their entire character instead of just the specific behavior or thought process that led to the failure. Such tendencies can seriously upset their self-confidence. Instead of fostering self-criticism, it's crucial to teach your child the power of self-evaluation. So, what's the difference? When self-criticizing, they only dwell on what went wrong and attach negative labels to themselves, like "lazy" or "incompetent." In contrast, self-evaluation is a more constructive approach. It involves acknowledging shortcomings while reflecting on ways to improve and prevent the recurrence of mistakes.

This shift is vital for building confidence because it enables them to rebound from failures and strive for success in their future attempts. Every child, regardless of shyness or anxiety, has the potential to become a self-confident individual. With the right guidance and unwavering support from their parents, these kids can boost their confidence in all aspects of life. Encourage your highly sensitive child to communicate with others, build strong relationships, step out of their comfort zones, and follow their life goals. Remind them that mistakes are part of learning and growing, and self-evaluation empowers them to overcome challenges and become more confident individuals. With your guidance, they'll gain the resilience and self-assurance needed to navigate life's journey with confidence and determination.

As you raise your highly sensitive children, keep in mind that one day, they will venture out into the world on their own.

While this might feel overwhelming, the best thing you can do is equip them with the tools they need to thrive independently. Remember, you are their guide and support system, preparing them to face the world with strength and self-assurance.

7

SCHOOL AND EDUCATIONAL SUPPORT

Your child spends half of their time at school learning and socializing with their classmates. If their school isn't an accommodating place that understands and supports their needs, they will struggle, and their grades will fall behind.

Schools don't only influence your child's academic development but their emotional and mental growth as well. In fact, just like family, school has a huge impact on your child's behavior and well-being. For this reason, parents of highly sensitive children should exert extra effort to find the right educational setting for their little ones.

Highly sensitive children have different needs from sensitive children, so you should look for schools that cater to your kid's specific needs. This chapter discusses challenges and opportunities your child may face in school, how to choose the right educational environment for them, and how you can support their social and academic success.

Challenges and Opportunities in Educational Settings

The school environment can pose both opportunities and challenges for highly sensitive children. It gives them a chance to learn, express themselves, and interact with people their age. They can also provide challenges like a loud environment, constant distractions, and teachers who don't understand their specific needs. Parents should be aware of both and choose a school that can provide their child with more opportunities than challenges.

Challenges Highly Sensitive Children Face in School

Chaotic classrooms can be a nightmare for highly sensitive children. Since they pick up on every detail in their environment, they can often feel overwhelmed. Constant movements, loud noises, strange scents, bad lighting, uncomfortable uniforms, and other types of overstimulation can be hard on your child. They can also struggle in group projects or activities. Highly sensitive children have overly active minds, which can make it hard to work with others, as they prefer to think and brainstorm alone. They are also deep thinkers, so they need peace and quiet and to take their time to process their thoughts. As a result, they can struggle with keeping up with their peers in group activities.

There are usually about twenty children in a classroom, and each experiences different emotions. Your child is absorbing these feelings all day which can overwhelm them and drain their energy.

Similar to schools, teachers can either make your child's life easier or more difficult. For instance, they can give their students negative feedback instead of constructive criticism. This can affect children differently depending on their level of sensitivity.

Some will listen to their teacher's comments and work harder and thrive, while others can feel discouraged. However, highly sensitive children will be extremely frustrated and disappointed in themselves.

One of the biggest challenges your child will face is bullies. Bullying is destructive and can damage any child's self-esteem and cause them anxiety, depression, and other mental issues. So, can you imagine its impact on highly sensitive children? Even if your child doesn't get bullied, they will still pick up on the negative vibes and the pain of bullied children. The injustice and ill-treatment that their peers are subjected to every day can affect them. In time, they will hate going to school, and their academic progress will deteriorate.

Although your child should make friends and expand their social circle, they can feel uncomfortable in large groups. Your empathetic child may struggle with separating themselves from their mates' issues. For instance, if some of their friends are going through a tough time, your little one will feel that these problems are theirs as well, which can overwhelm them and increase their stress.

Some children also like to make fun of their friends without meaning to be ill-spirited, while others can be cruel. Either way, your child will not handle harsh words well, whether they are jokes or not, and can be deeply hurt.

Opportunities for Highly Sensitive Children in School

Schools provide children with the opportunity to learn and grow in their education. Highly sensitive children are equally highly creative. School introduces them to various artistic outlets like art, music, or acting. Since your child can't easily communicate their emotions, creative outlets give them a chance to express their complex emotions.

If your child has an understanding teacher, they can encourage them to work hard by providing constructive criticism and positive feedback. Your child will also meet other highly sensitive kids at school. Being around like-minded people who understand what they are going through can be beneficial and make them feel less alone. They can also interact with different people and work on their social skills. Your child can also observe how other children react in different situations and learn how to express their feelings properly.

School also teaches your child structure, organization, and how to follow the rules. It is necessary your child learns these things at an early age so they can benefit in the future. One of the greatest things schools do for children is introduce them to books, which can become their refuge when they feel overwhelmed or stressed; they can get lost in a book to calm themselves down.

Supporting Your Child's Academic and Social Success

School won't always be easy for your child. However, when you support them and care for their needs, they will flourish and thrive.

Explain They Aren't Alone

Your child is aware they are different even if they don't say it out loud. They will probably dread school because they are worried about being different or being judged by other kids. Before your child starts school, tell them about all the famous, highly sensitive people, whether they are real or fictional. For instance, you can watch "The Beauty and the Beast" together and point out how Belle is just like them. She is empathetic and different from everyone else in the village, but this makes her special, and she is able to see the Beast's true nature that is hidden behind his frightening appearance. You can also tell your child about Martin Luther King Jr, who was also highly sensitive. And used his special gift to bring justice to black people. You can use as many examples as you want to prepare your child. Remind them they will most likely meet other children like them at school, and they can be friends and bond over their unique abilities.

Remind Them of Their Strength

If your child thinks that their sensitivity is a weakness, this could impact their progress in school. Many parents also use terms like too sensitive or shy when describing their child, and without realizing it, they are affecting their child, causing them to believe that they don't have the same skills as their peers. As a result, they won't participate in a class or take the initiative in anything.

Your child needs to know that their strength lies in their high sensitivity. Explain to them that they can use their unique ability to make friends in school and see things that their peers can't. For instance, if they are studying a story, your child can use their empathy to understand the characters' pain and struggles unlike anyone else in the class.

Tell them to use their emotional intelligence to make friends. Other kids will love their empathy and ability to sense when they are sad and need a sympathetic ear. Simply put, make your child believe that their high sensitivity is their superpower, and they should be proud of it and embrace it.

Plan Playdates with Your Child's Peers

Playdates will give your child a chance to know their classmates in a familiar and relaxing environment. When your child feels comfortable around them, they will approach them in class and strike up a conversation. Playdates will also improve their social skills and make them feel at ease around other children.

However, if your child feels uncomfortable with socialization, don't push them, or they will dread any type of group interaction in the future. Observe your child's energy and temperament, and organize play dates only when they feel energetic and in a good mood.

Taking Breaks

Recess provides children with time to relax, eat, catch up with their friends, and take a break from schoolwork. However, your child can feel overwhelmed and stressed during this time. They are in a chaotic environment surrounded by loud kids and food smells. Tell your child to do whatever makes them comfortable during recess. If they want to sit with their friends and talk, they should do that. However, if they need to decompress, suggest they spend time in the library where they can read or paint. They can also take noise-canceling headphones to school and wear them when they need peace and quiet.

Make sure they have some alone time at home as well. Encourage them to do whatever they want, like watching TV, painting, or playing a game when they get home from school. This will calm them down and make them feel refreshed before they do their homework. If the first thing your child does when they get home is to study, they won't be able to focus.

Provide Reassurance

Your child probably struggles with approaching kids their age and making friends. Many children can be outgoing and have already established their own social groups. This can make it harder for your child because they have to approach a group of people rather than just one person and risk rejection. As a result, your child will often feel frustrated.

Talk to your child about their feelings. However, don't ask them right away if they have made friends or not. Tell them to mention three good things about their day and three bad things. If they tell you they are struggling with meeting new people, validate their feelings. Remind them of all the times they succeeded in adjusting to new situations and developing friendships. You may be tempted to find friends for them, but this isn't helpful. Let your child navigate the social world themselves and learn the necessary skills.

Choosing an Educational Environment for Your Child

There are certain aspects that every parent should look for when choosing a school for their child.

· The principal and teachers should have a background in developing psychology

· Teachers must have the necessary training to deal with highly sensitive children

· They should be able to recognize a highly sensitive child right away

· There should be two teachers in the class

· There should be highly sensitive teachers in school or at least understand what it means to be highly sensitive and how it affects your child

· Teachers who accept sensitivity without judgment

· Teachers should be compassionate, kind, and patient

· Teachers shouldn't shout or raise their voices in class

· Teachers should exert effort to focus on children who have specific needs

· Teachers should be willing to talk to their students, get to know them, and learn about their personalities, skills, and interests

· Teachers should make every kid in the class feel heard and seen

· The school should provide a safe environment for children to express their needs and expectations from their teachers and school

· Highly sensitive children should be notified in advance when teachers decide to change their seating arrangements

· The environment in class should be comfortable without any bright lights or distracting drawings

· No clutter and only minimal decorations in class

· Structured and quiet classrooms

· Schools should feel cozy like home, not like an institution

· A slow-paced environment

· Children are given the opportunity to unwind when they feel overwhelmed

· The school should provide comfortable reading spaces.

· Children should learn relaxation techniques and self-compassion

· They should learn to accept their emotions

· Schools should focus on children's well-being before their academic progress

There are also a few questions that you should ask the school before making a decision.

- How does the school communicate with the parents?

- How do they handle discipline?

- What is the school's learning style and environment?

- How do they plan to support and accommodate highly sensitive children?

- How many students are in class?

Once you choose a school, talk with the teachers and staff about your child's needs. Don't shy away from speaking up whenever your child has a bad experience at school, such as when they feel overstimulated or are seated in a noisy spot, and address your concerns right away. If the child returns home not feeling like themselves, talk to their teachers to find out what happened at school. Give the school your email and number so they can contact you with any questions or concerns.

Accommodations and Modifications to Facilitate Your Child's Learning

There are certain things you can do at home or suggestions you can make to your teachers to facilitate your child's learning.

Talk to Their Teachers

Although there is often more than one highly sensitive child in every classroom in America, don't assume that the teacher or principal knows about high sensitivity. Before your child begins school, talk to them, and explain how your child should be treated.

Classroom Changes

Your sensitive child is most likely introverted. Introverts need alone time during the day to recharge. Your child can also feel overwhelmed by their emotions and will need to spend time by themselves to calm down. This can be impossible in a classroom filled with over twenty children. You can suggest to their principal or teacher to have a private space for your child to unwind. Many schools will accommodate your request since there are most likely other highly sensitive students in class, and the seating arrangements can be overwhelming for them.

For instance, in many elementary schools in America, students are seated at round tables to have discussions and allow all children to participate. This activity can either encourage your child to take part and get out of their comfort zone or feel uncomfortable because they hate being the center of attention. This can depend on their temperament and mood.

Most highly sensitive children prefer sitting on individual desks where they can have their own space and privacy. Don't hesitate to talk to their teacher to change the seating arrangement and suggest they come up with different activities that suit all personality types, including highly sensitive and introverted kids.

For instance, teachers can have a corner in class where highly sensitive children can work in peace whenever they feel overwhelmed and can't handle overstimulation.

You can also assign a small space at home for your child whenever you feel overwhelmed and place coloring books, crayons, story books, games, toys, and anything else that they will enjoy. They can also use this space to unwind after school.

Different Learning Styles

Explain to your child's teacher their learning style and that there are certain things that make them uncomfortable. For instance, some teachers can push children to participate in class to get them out of their comfort zone. However, this technique won't work with highly sensitive children who don't like to be put on the spot. Your child will also need time to arrange their thoughts before answering a question. Ask their teacher not to rush them and to give them time to think.

Mention Your Child's Strength

If your child is shy, introverted, and doesn't participate much in class, they won't be on the teacher's radar or receive any feedback from them. Ask the teacher to observe your child in class, take notes of their strengths and unique skills, and constantly mention them to the child. Tell the teacher that your child's sensitivity has provided them with many unique qualities like empathy, observation, deep thinking, thoughtfulness, and deep listening. They need to see your child as more than a highly sensitive kid.

The right school environment is essential for your highly sensitive child's well-being. Find the ideal school and talk with the teachers and staff in advance to make sure they accommodate your child's needs. If they can't, look for another school. The right educational setting can make your child grow and be the best version of themselves.

8

PARENTING STRATEGIES FOR DIFFERENT DEVELOPMENTAL STAGES

Each stage of a child's development comes with different challenges and opportunities. For the same reasons, parenting strategies for highly sensitive children should be tailored to their current developmental stage. This chapter provides guidance for the three main stages of children's development: early childhood, middle childhood, and adolescence. For each age group, you'll receive age-specific advice and guidance for addressing the distinct needs and characteristics of highly sensitive children at that specific stage and effective parenting strategies that promote your child's development, emotional well-being, and autonomy.

The Best Strategies for Early Childhood

Older toddlers and children up to the age of seven have unique needs when it comes to overcoming sensitivity. In toddlerhood, children begin seeking autonomy yet rely on their parents for guidance and meeting basic needs. Even after the age of three, kids are still learning how to regulate their emotions, which makes sensitivity-inducing challenges even harder to combat.

On top of that, they can't understand the concept of emotions, so parents often have a hard time helping them self-regulate in challenging situations. However, the following tips and emotional regulation strategies for working through things with your kid will set you on the path of navigating even the most intimidating environments.

Connecting and Validating their Feelings

Like many other young kids with heightened sensitivity, your child might feel you won't understand their reactions, or worse; you'll dismiss them. The most effective strategy for teaching them how to handle big emotions is to connect with them and validate their reactions. Let's say an older relative told your child they have big ears. They've meant it as a lighthearted comment, a joke - but your child took it seriously and burst out crying. In this situation, ask your child why that comment hurt them. Let them tell you how it made them feel in their own words. They might be unable to express their emotions, so listen to whatever way they express, being uncomfortable, sad, angry, etc. Tell them you understand why they reacted the way they did to validate their feelings. Knowing you won't dismiss them will raise their confidence and jumpstart their self-regulation journey. Once they see they can turn to you for support when dealing with big feelings, it will be easier to teach them the necessary coping, self-soothing, and distress-tolerating strategies.

Spending Time with Your Child

Young kids are impressionable and learn a lot by modeling their parent's behavior. On the other hand, by spending regular one-on-one time with your child, you can learn a great deal about them too. Just playing with them for 15 minutes without distractions can give tremendous insight into their little personalities and provide an avenue for choosing the best approach to their parenting. After all, all children have unique traits, and you must tailor your techniques based on your kiddo's needs. This time should be spent away from electronic screens and conversations with others, so the child can have her undivided attention. Look for an activity your child enjoys, nurturing their individuality. This type of positive attention will foster their social and emotional development and provide a fantastic bonding experience between parent and child. Remember, spending time with their parents is just as critical for children's parenting as discipline, routines, and guidance through emotional hurdles.

Preparing for Every Situation

While this is true for all children, overly sensitive kids thrive on well-established routines and consistency. They want to know what to expect in any situation because it gives them a sense of control they don't have in their inner world. By meeting this need, you can help them adapt to new environments and cope better with challenging situations. Another way you can help your child prepare for stressful situations is to role-play different scenarios. Help them come up with ways to calm themselves when they feel overwhelmed and relieve anxiety in a socially acceptable way. For example, you can teach them to start breathing deeply whenever they feel those big emotions flare up. Or, if they need to express their feelings physically (which is common in young children), you can show them how to do it by lightly stomping on the ground or kneading a handful of play dough.

Setting Boundaries and a Safe Space

Your child is more sensitive to the input they receive from their environment and more likely to react to it. With a few simple steps, you can prevent them from getting triggered. For toddlers and infants, this means keeping whatever area they spend the most time in a trigger-free zone. For instance, if loud noises trigger your child, don't raise the volume around them. For ages four to seven, establish a safe zone for downtime after stimulating activities. Don't schedule several similar activities one after another. You can also explain to your child the concept of boundaries by saying, "If you tell me what makes you upset, I'll try my best not to do that." Or, you can say, "If you feel upset, you can go to your room until you calm down." The goal is to give them space and time to safely process the big feelings.

Practicing Discipline, the Right Way

One of the major hurdles parents of overly sensitive kids encounter is disciplining a child that gets upset whenever they feel uncomfortable. Your child will likely criticize themselves if they've done something wrong, so you must tread very carefully when administering punishment. Be gentle and communicate clearly. Explain the limits they've crossed but emphasize that you aren't judging them. Avoid using negative descriptions of their behavior and take the "actions have consequences" approach instead. For instance, if your child refuses to eat their dinner, tell them they won't have playtime because they didn't eat when everybody else did - rather than telling them they can't play because they behaved poorly during dinner.

Tips for Parenting in Middle Childhood

Parenting a highly sensitive older child also comes with special considerations. At this age, your child has already developed their personality, likes, and dislikes and understands certain concepts like feelings, emotional regulation, and social skills. Here, the focus shifts to adjusting your discipline approach to match your kid's temperament. Below are some handy parenting strategies that address your kiddo's unique needs in middle childhood.

Enabling Downtime

Older kids with heightened sensitivity need a lot of downtime too. Your child can be easily overwhelmed by everyday activities like participating in class, sports, and other non-school-related activities. The sounds and other stimuli can overload their senses, so avoiding stacking activities and ensuring quiet time in between is a great way to relieve their burden. For example, instead of scheduling a sports activity right after school, get them home first for a little time to recharge their mental energy. They will enjoy their sports activity more if they don't have to deal with processing stimuli from before too.

Praising and Motivating

With a little help, children in elementary or lower middle school classes can catch up on emotional regulation skills faster than younger kids. When they manage to cope with a trigger, praise them enthusiastically to encourage similar behavior in the future. Conversely, if you see them working through a complex issue and struggling, provide a few suggestions on how to use their strengths. Let's say they feel upset because their friend said something they interpreted as rude or hurtful. Encourage your child to tap into their emphatic skills by asking themselves what made their friends say those words. Did they have a disagreement, or was the friend hurt because they failed a test or were punished by their parents? Considering the different possibilities will motivate them to acknowledge their and others' emotions and develop better-coping mechanisms for similar events in the future.

Teaching Emotions

Because your child understands the concept of emotions, you can teach them what different sentiments look like by describing or role-playing specific situations. That way, you can get them to understand and express their feelings. For example, you can bring up an incident when they had a meltdown because they had to wear their blue sweater instead of the green one. Put on a piece of clothing that you feel doesn't match your outfit and explain how it makes you feel. Then encourage your kid to do the same.

Gaining Insight into Your Own Temperament

By the time they reach school age, your child has developed the majority of their fundamental personality traits. Comparing their personality to yours, you're likely to discover many similarities and differences between them and yourself. Looking into your own temperament and preferences might provide a clue on what your child needs to thrive. For example, if you prefer to work or wind down in a less stimulating environment and your child displays similar preferences, you'll already have your answers. Conversely, if your child's needs differ from yours, looking into the differences will help you understand how to communicate with your sensitive child.

Disciplining

Understanding your child's temperament will also help you come up with discipline that helps their abilities evolve. Now that they're at an age where they can express their emotions better, it's even more crucial to acknowledge their feelings. Letting you know what they feel doesn't mean they understand why they feel that way, much less how to cope with those emotions. However, by validating their sentiments, you're fostering their emotional awareness.

Show empathy and have a positive attitude when disciplining your child. For example, if you're punishing your kid for not doing their homework, mention that they were doing a good job finishing their homework lately. Tell them that you know they were tired and forgot to do their homework, but they still have to do it anyway - or face the consequences. Then, provide feedback by explaining that by doing it on time, they won't have to worry about it (or the punishment) later. Avoid raising your voice so they can focus on the message instead of getting distracted by the harsh sound coming from your mouth.

Dealing with Highly Sensitive Adolescents

After toddlerhood, adolescence is the second major milestone in your child's life. At this age, they will try to establish a higher level of independence, at the same time as being confronted with a growing number of expectations. Despite knowing how to communicate their emotions, many teenagers don't like to speak about their feelings to their parents or caregivers because they don't think they will be understood. Below are some effective strategies for parenting overly sensitive adolescents and helping them become confident and happy adults.

Talking about Your Own Emotions

If your teen is reluctant to talk about their feelings, you can break the ice by talking to them about yours. Don't be afraid to tell them you're frustrated because you forgot to buy something at the supermarket or upset after a work project didn't come out as planned. It will help your teen normalize emotions and see that you're aware of yours. It prompts them to develop healthier relationships with their own feelings. Express your feelings and model a constructive way of dealing with them to teach your teen to identify and regulate their own feelings. If they see you aren't ashamed of your negative emotions, they won't feel stigmatized about theirs, and their self-confidence will soar.

Teens are more likely to home in on expressing emotions during stressful situations rather than focusing on how to avoid or resolve the issue. They're still learning to cope with stressors and might not know how to manage triggers yet. This is another reason parents are crucial models of how to cope with stress. You can show them how you set boundaries and deal with stress through exercise and relaxation techniques, seeking support, and engaging in self-care.

Building Their Self Esteem

Another way to raise your sensitive teenager's self-esteem is to boost their personal competence. Praise and reward your teen for effectively managing stressors and teach them better skills if they struggle to cope with triggers. For these teens, every negative word can seem like a personal attack, which will have adverse effects on their self-confidence. Instead, encourage your teen to work on their strengths by identifying positive emotions. For example, you can ask them to think back about a challenging situation they had recently. Encourage them to tell you what they found positive in that experience. Did they have fun before they were confronted with the trigger? If they did, they could focus on that next time instead of letting the trigger run their day - or worse, make them avoid the situation/experience altogether.

Allow Them to Be Seen and Heard

Due to the growing number of social and academic expectations, sensitive teens often feel overwhelmed by the sheer amount of information they must process day after day. Feeling like they must fill all these expectations when they already find coping with so many stimuli incredibly difficult can make them feel unheard (which, in turn, leads to exaggerated reactions). You can validate their concerns and teach them how to overcome their difficulties by making them feel seen and heard. Active listening, repeating what they're saying, and offering empathic advice will go a long way in reassuring them that they aren't alone. If they know they can speak to you without facing criticism, your teen will be more willing to open up and convey their thoughts and feelings.

Don't Try to Shield Them from the Outside World

Keeping your child in a bubble will only reinforce their fears. Instead of trying to shield your extra-sensitive teen from the outside world, provide them with effective coping strategies and emotional regulation skills. While they need a supportive and safe environment for processing big emotions, they must also be exposed to a broad range of experiences. Through these, they learn how to face challenges head-on and manage their emotions more effectively.

Some of the most effective coping techniques for teens are expressing emotions through art, music, or any other non-verbal way, seeking support from friends, self-soothing strategies like breathing and quick meditation exercises, positive thinking strategies (positive affirmations), cognitive reframing (trying to look at the positive aspect of the situation instead of the negative one) and acceptance of one's emotions.

Before exposing your teen to a new experience, ask them what they think about it. If they feel scared, ask them to rate their fear on a scale of 1-10. If their fear rates are lower than three, encourage them to take on the challenge. If it's lower than six, help them devise coping strategies in case their emotions get out of control. Meanwhile, if their fear level is higher than seven, they should avoid that situation.

After exposure and during practice, ask your teen to reflect on their feelings so that they can understand them. Encourage them to see the advantages and disadvantages of each emotion.

Disciplining Teens

The best way to discipline an overly sensitive adolescent is to lay out clear rules and the consequences if they break them. Doing this can help you avoid making your teen feel criticized and ashamed instead of teaching them about actions and consequences. Harsh words and criticism only damage their already shaky self-esteem. Despite their desire to be independent, your teen is still looking to you to navigate the world, and if they see you upset with them, yelling, and using harsh discipline, they will reinforce their self-deprecating thoughts. Positive reinforcement and gentle guidance, on the other hand, encourage positive thoughts, emotions, and behavior.

Avoiding Power Struggles

Teenagers often seek to establish autonomy, which often leads to power struggles between parent and child, putting another layer of stress on their already strained mental health. To void this, you should provide a safe place for them at home. If you notice your teen has problems, use a respectful approach to help them identify and resolve their issues. Listen to them actively, show empathy for their plight, and be ready to compromise if the solution requires it. It will make your teen feel validated and foster their independence. While you shouldn't disregard rules and boundaries to avoid power struggles, providing options will be a great alternative. For an extra-sensitive teen, even a simple choice as deciding when to do a chore can give them the control, they need to manage their emotions. It fosters self-confidence and self-efficacy, which results in empowered emotional well-being and a fierce sense of self in adolescents.

9

ENHANCING SOCIAL SKILLS AND RELATIONSHIPS

Highly sensitive children are very aware of their surroundings. They possess many unique characteristics that set them apart from the average kid. They give more expression to emotions, are empathetic, and are a little more curious than the norm. Unlike other kids, your sensitive child would likely take things more 'personally' and suffer guilt and regret for even the barest feeling of failure or condemnation. This will greatly impact their social lives and how they view those around them. They tread extra carefully while observing the feelings of people around them. When they feel they're not welcome, they do everything in their power to not upset the other party.

Your sensitive child may be shy or fearful, especially when they have an introverted temperament. Although this might not be their true identity, they need to feel loved and supported by their parents and those around them so they can express their real traits freely. As a parent, you must pay keen interest and attention to your child's emotions and behavior. It's your role to teach them healthy ways to express themselves, come out of their shells, and socialize. Parenting a highly sensitive child can be challenging. In their daily lives, they take the little, barely noticed details and agonize over them. They get easily overwhelmed and worry a lot about getting into people's bad books; they cry and feel emotions easily and, due to this, need constant reassurance. When they feel extreme emotions like anger, happiness, sadness, or fear, it is difficult for them to socialize and build relationships.

You can help your child build and maintain their social skills. Children need a means to express themselves, play, and be creative with kids their age. That's the only way they get to come out of their shells. In this chapter, you'll learn the keys and techniques to guide your child toward building healthy social skills. You'll also be taught the right strategies to support their development. By the end of this chapter, you will have been properly guided into how you can create a good social network for your child and even the entire family.

Building and Maintaining Your Child's Social Skills

Your child's sensitivity is more of a gift. Their mind can process and thoroughly analyze more information than the mind of a normal child. As your child becomes more aware of their environment, they can spot opportunities and threats around them. Their nervous system responds to reflexes faster, they feel pain more, and they are easily prone to allergens. This means that your child's physical, emotional, and psychological being will easily detect anything that comes into contact with it.

For this reason, your child will only want to mingle with those they feel less threatened around. They will value friends who have their best interests at heart. Observing such people around them wouldn't be hard, seeing that they notice the littlest details about people and things. A good friend is what your child needs. Their curiosity about their environment gives rise to their interest in many things. Your child may need a great deal of your attention to open up. As a parent, sometimes you feel that no matter how much time you spend with your highly sensitive child, it is never enough. In this journey of building their social skills, you may ask yourself these questions:

- What do I need to do more of to reach out to my kid?
- Why won't they socialize like every regular kid?
- What can I do to enhance their social skills?

You need to aim for a solid and secure parental relationship with your child. It enhances their self-confidence, social development, and emotional maturity. What you may not know is that your highly sensitive child wants to make friends and build relationships with others, but they find it difficult to adjust entirely to new circumstances and unfamiliar faces. They need to familiarize themselves more with the other kids. Otherwise, they may struggle to keep up with their peers. Sensitive children are more comfortable building or having a single, one-on-one interaction than with groups of children. They often avoid places that are overcrowded or have an unbearable level of noise. As you encourage them to come out more and socialize, ensure you do not enforce your will on them. They'll adjust with time and when they feel ready. An ideal situation would be if you were able to find a support group for highly sensitive children and organize socials together.

Tips and Strategies to Support Your Child's Social Development

Most times, let your kid follow a path they feel is right for them and make friendships along the way, but at other times, they may need a little more support and reassurance from you. When it comes to social development, there are many ways to lay the right foundation for helping them build successful friendships. Consider the following strategies:

Define a Real Friend

Highly sensitive children have many misconceptions about who or what a friend is. They can sometimes find it difficult to speak up for themselves and be taken advantage of. Being your child's number one friend and guide, you should set them on the right path. Define who a friend is and what role they should play in your kid's life. As you go about this, put it to them in a language they will understand. For example, a friend is someone who is willing to play with them and doesn't mind taking turns. A friend is someone who cares about their needs and cheers them up when they're down. Make your child understand that friendship means enjoying each other's company and time. While you teach them who a friend is, guide them on how they could also be better friends. They should never talk against or be mean; true friends encourage each other and care about each other's feelings.

Help Them Get Involved with Peers of Similar Interests

Schools have created systems where children or students must participate in group tasks or projects, for example, team sports, quizzes, and competitions. This may not sit well with your highly sensitive child, so don't force them into these activities. If they don't feel comfortable participating in group tasks, let them be. Your child will be happier when they find themselves in a space where they're involved in something they enjoy and are not pressured to do.

Give Them a Heads up Before Any Surprises

Sensitive children do not like surprises, so avoid them. If you are planning a visit to their favorite aunt or relative, ensure they are given a heads-up to feel more settled and in control of the situation. It benefits your sensitive child when they know what to expect in their daily activities and in life generally. Preparing them ahead of time would do them more good than harm. While you prepare with them, you can throw out some very common questions you feel will come up on a visit, for example, what's your name? Where are you from? What's your favorite color? What's your best meal? Make sure they're well aware of the answers to these questions.

Live as an Example of Good Social Behavior

One of the best ways to grow your child's social skills is to teach them by example. Children often learn by seeing. You cannot be bad at something and expect them to thrive in that field. This would make you put your social skills to work more if you previously didn't. Show and teach your sensitive child some social skills; sharing opinions is more graceful than imposing them, taking turns, knowing when to lose, and accepting loss is more important than feeling anger and sadness at losses. When you continually teach these life techniques, you'll be amazed at how well they begin to enjoy positive relationships with their peers.

Another way to set a good example is by guiding them toward the right skills and passion. You can encourage them to participate in certain activities, for example, learning a musical instrument, acting, or playing voiceovers.

Partner with Them and Be Patient with Them

There's so much your child can offer you and those around them. Their good observation skills make them more careful and precise while making decisions. Their ability to weigh options and give deep thought to something before taking action saves them the stress of painful experiences. Your child needs your help making the right decision about their best friend. Partnering with your child and being their advocate and biggest support during social connections creates a happier and safer space for more of their expressions. Remember, your child processes emotions more deeply than others, and they can see what others cannot because of their observation skills - all the more reason why partnering, with a sprinkle of patience, works well when dealing with them.

Addressing Social Challenges Faced by Highly Sensitive Children

Highly sensitive children may face unique social challenges, especially social anxiety, difficulties with peer interaction, and so on. You should be readily available to encourage your child and help them through this growth stage. Here are some strategies that would help address such issues:

Help Validate Their Feelings

It's necessary to help your child through any anxiety in the social world. Let them know that their feelings and opinions are valid and understood. Sometimes sensitive kids find it difficult to express their opinions since they've never been heard outside their safe space; this makes them feel that whatever they say isn't important and should be kept inside. Make them know this idea is false, and they have as much right to speak their minds as anyone else. This will help them build trust and confidence in themselves.

Teach Them How to Regulate Their Emotions

Teach your child how to express basic emotions like anger, pain, joy, and sadness more appropriately. For example, they must never yell at anyone when angry, take it on anyone when sad or in pain, or awkwardly over-express their joy. Teach them to practice coping mechanisms like deep breathing in and out; this will help them manage their stress and anxiety levels. You should also teach them to identify triggers for those emotions and implement measures to manage or avoid them.

Create a Safe and Supportive Space for Them

Many highly sensitive children like a space where they're accepted, loved, and cared for. Sometimes they recharge by being alone. You must recognize this and respect their privacy when they need to be alone after being overwhelmed by an issue, respect that, and let them heal.

Put Yourself in Their Shoes

When you put yourself in your child's social circumstances, you'll come to understand why certain things play out the way they do. For instance, one of your coworkers invites you to an event. Right there, you see some 'colleagues' who are unfamiliar to you. Your friend then urges you to speak to them because they relate well to them and expect you to do the same. How would you feel or respond to this? Remember that your child doesn't have the same coping skills or mechanisms as you, so pushing them does more harm than good. They might not tell you how uncomfortable they feel and just do as they're told, but you should be aware of when your child feels comfortable with situations and when they don't.

Encourage Healthy Hobbies and Exposures

Children have hobbies, which include playing games, singing, watching their favorite TV shows, and many more. You can guide them into creating healthy hobbies that will help them connect with like-minded kids. When interacting with like-minded kids, they will feel more comfortable expressing themselves, making their social interactions more fun and meaningful. It also works well, giving them gradual exposure to social activities, for example, by holding a small birthday party where only families and those they're familiar with get to attend. This would help them feel less overwhelmed.

Your child is unique, and their progress in social development may take a while. Be their best friend and support partner, exercise patience, and celebrate their little achievements.

Encourage Positive Social Interaction: Fostering Empathy, Kindness, and Effective Communication

Teach your child to reflect empathy and kindness towards others and use this to help them build effective communication skills. Here are strategies to help with that:

The Process Begins with You

To encourage your child's social interaction, you must first consider your expectations as a parent and manage them. You might think that in this social development journey, your major role would be to encourage and assist them into freedom, but it goes deeper than that. Most parents want their children to live up to their expectations of a perfect child. They want their child to achieve what they couldn't at a young age. Watching your child try to strive socially can get frustrating if they don't live up to your ideals. They may not even want to make an effort, and you might have to push and encourage them a lot. Remember that patience is a virtue that always pays off and that your child is different from you and will have their own developmental timeframe. Your child may not show it, but they look up to you for guidance, and it's up to you to lead them to a life of empathy, kindness, and confidence. Effective communication begins with how you speak to them or the people around you. If they must follow, then they must watch you do it first.

Teach Empathy and Kindness

Help your sensitive child understand what empathy and kindness mean. Teach them to recognize and respect the emotions of others. To make this practical, try teaching them through scenes in movies, books, short plays, or events. When they recognize emotions and know what follows them, they can better respond to them. You should also encourage them to view the world through the lenses of others and not just through their own eyes. Ask questions like, "How do you think that person felt when .... happened?"

Be an Active Listener

Teach them the importance of listening attentively while others speak. You can practice this while you talk to them. When you're both in a short argument, show them that you respect their opinions and let them finish making a point before you speak. They should also follow suit. Also, encourage eye contact and the right posture to show their level of engagement while in a conversation.

Groom Them with a Culture of Kindness at Home

There's no better place to learn good manners than at home. You owe them that responsibility to always show kindness and empathy towards people, even amongst their peers. Teach them to forgive when they're wronged.

Importance of Creating a Supportive Social Network for Your Child and Family

Here are some reasons why your child should build a strong social network within and outside the family:

· Sense of Belonging: Being part of a support group helps them get some relief when they feel left out and alone. Children want to feel loved, valued, and appreciated, which helps them feel secure and increases self-worth and confidence.

· A good network helps your child through emotional challenges. When they have friends and relatives to turn to when they're down, it helps them through difficult times. An understanding group can also help them cope with stress and difficult situations.

· A good social network reduces your child's isolation. Keeping them in full isolation may not be a good idea because you're trying to respect their space. Teach them how to come out often and interact with others to build their confidence level and help them better express their emotions.

Sensitive children have difficulty keeping up with their environment and society. They see and feel more than normal children, which often leads to them becoming isolated and introverted. As a parent, you are your child's first lifeguard in the real world; you're the one to help them through these developmental stages and give them opportunities to express themselves more.

10

SUPPORTING ACADEMIC SUCCESS

Supporting a highly sensitive child academically can pose quite a challenge for parents because these kids do not respond the same way as regular children when they are disciplined. Of course, ensuring that your kid is well-adjusted means disciplining them when needed, but because highly sensitive children feel things on a deeper level, the traditional techniques do not work well for them. Plus, punishing your highly sensitive kid for something that is beyond their control could send them the wrong message.

For instance, a highly sensitive person will break down crying or have a meltdown when they feel overwhelmed or are in the middle of a sensory breakdown. If you react badly to this behavior, your child will become even more closed off from you. Instead, you need to give them time and space to recover from being overstimulated. Some parents think this behavior is because their kid is just shy or timid, and they can phase it out by disciplining them; however, this misconception couldn't be more wrong. This not only mislabels highly sensitive children but also increases the problems they are facing with their academics.

Though you can be strict and assertive with your highly sensitive kid, you should never be harsh. They feel things deeply, and hurtful behavior will only make their progress much slower. It doesn't help that most schools are not very progressive when it comes to dealing with special needs children and treat them like all other children. This is why your child needs your help more than ever, especially with their studies. It's likely they are suffering and not telling anyone. What you can do is make sure they have a teacher who understands the unique needs of your HSC and is willing to go the extra mile for them.

In addition, you should aim to create a conducive learning environment at home that encourages your child to work better. Find out about the different learning styles and try to leverage your child's strengths. Finally, while you help them with their academics, it's crucial that you don't forget about their emotional well-being in the process. This chapter will help you achieve all of this and more, so keep on reading.

Acknowledge High Sensitivity as a Trait

If you want to really help your highly sensitive child, you first need to acknowledge and understand their condition. High sensitivity should not be classified as a mental disorder but rather as a personality trait. Let your child know that it's okay to be sensitive, even if their fellow students don't understand this yet. It would also be great if a teacher at their school also knew how to recognize a highly sensitive child and understands how to effectively deal with them. Take time to help your child consider this trait a positive aspect of their personality instead of weakness or vulnerability. This will essentially help you foster a sense of self-acceptance and confidence within your young one, which, in turn, will help them to be more focused on their studies instead of being self-conscious in class.

Gentle and Caring Attitude

When it comes to poor performance or misbehavior in class or during studying, it's essential that you take a gentle and caring approach with your HSC. Be constructive, assertive, and firm, but do not raise your voice. Don't make groundless accusations like, "You never pay attention in class," "You're just lazy and don't put in any effort," "You always make the same mistakes over and over again," or, "You don't care about your grades or your future." Instead, you should provide positive and constructive statements that help your child work to their strengths. For instance, you could say, "I've noticed that sometimes it's hard for you to pay attention in class. Let's find fun ways to help you stay focused and learn better", "Sometimes studying can be tough. Let's come up with a schedule together and try different study tricks to make it easier and more enjoyable", "We all make mistakes when learning new things. Let's practice those areas together and find ways to improve", or "I know you care about doing well in school and thinking about the future can be overwhelming. Let's talk about your dreams and make a plan to achieve them, one step at a time".

Knowledge in Mindfulness

The best way to help your HSC avoid mistakes and errors in their work is to incorporate mindfulness into their routines. The practice of mindfulness keeps you grounded in the present moment and increases your focus on what you're doing. Highly sensitive children are prone to getting distracted while studying, solving a problem, or writing. Practicing mindfulness will help them become more aware of what they're studying or doing at the moment rather than being distracted by others. You can try different mindfulness activities like mindfulness meditation, body scans, sensory exercises, breathing techniques, etc.

Find a Good School

Finding a good school for your HSC is extremely important if you want to see them progress academically at a good pace. The overall school environment should be quiet and cozy; this should be a place that is similar to their home. The environment shouldn't have too much visual clutter or bright lights, as this can cause overstimulation. The class size should be relatively small so the teacher can focus on each student individually and monitor their progress. All these factors impact how a highly sensitive child performs in a class. Ensure you also talk to the teacher about the seating arrangement and keep them seated away from unruly or noisy children. If there are noise-canceling headphones for reading rooms and quiet time, that would be perfect for HSCs. They should have regular breaks between classes to process their thoughts and recover from stimulation instead of having consecutive classes all day.

Dealing with Perfectionism

Highly sensitive children are deeply aware of the criticism and praise they get, which is why they try their best to do everything right. This becomes a compulsive need to perfect each and every part of their life, including academics. At the same time, they are also susceptible to overstimulation, making it difficult to focus on what they're learning. As a result, they often struggle with their grades and test scores. This makes them feel insecure about their abilities. On top of this, if parents and teachers constantly compare and criticize highly sensitive kids, their self-esteem takes a considerable blow, and they start to get even worse.

This is why you should understand and accept that your HSC's test scores and grades do not reflect their true aptitudes and abilities. The traditional testing methods generally used to evaluate the performance of regular children are often unsuitable for sensitive children. These kids need to be relaxed when they're being tested and not rushed. This will only make them take more time than needed to answer questions and doubt themselves at every turn. You should also talk to the teacher about the school's testing methods to accommodate your child's unique learning needs. Or, the least they could do is offer calming activities before the exam. You can also do this by yourself before your child leaves for school every day.

In addition, you should let your child know that it's completely okay to struggle sometimes and that you're there to support them whenever they need it. It's best to establish that perfectionism isn't something that's essential to leading a happy, successful life. Encourage a growth mindset, which means embracing the idea that mistakes and setbacks are opportunities for learning and growth. Help them understand that making errors is a natural part of the learning process and does not define their worth or abilities. Teach them the value of self-compassion and the ability to treat themselves with kindness and understanding.

Give Them Regular Breaks

Overstimulation is one of the most common problems that highly sensitive children struggle with during their studies. The rapid pace of modern education, filled with bright visuals and other sensory input, can hinder their ability to concentrate on work. To help them get through overstimulation, you should first be able to recognize the signs and how you can handle them in an appropriate manner. HSCs need about 20 minutes to get through overstimulation, so it's best to take breaks when you see them getting overwhelmed. Alternatively, you could try to prevent overstimulation by giving them breaks between their studies to decompress, regain their energy, and focus for the next lesson. The signs of overstimulation include:

· **Daydreaming or "Spacing Out":** Your child might seem lost in thought or not fully present, like they're in their own little world.

·**Restlessness or Fidgeting**: They may have trouble sitting still and constantly moving around or playing with objects to release excess energy.

· **Sensitivity to Sounds**: Even everyday noises can bother them when they're overwhelmed. They might cover their ears, cringe, or show discomfort in response to certain sounds.

·**Irritability or Emotional Outbursts**: Overstimulation can make them easily irritated or set off emotional outbursts, like getting angry, crying, or having tantrums that seem out of proportion.

· **Avoidance Behaviors:** When they're overwhelmed, they may try to escape or avoid situations, places, or activities that they find overwhelming or too stimulating.

· **Physical Complaints:** They might complain about headaches, stomach aches, and feeling tired or show signs of physical tension like clenched fists or tight muscles.

·**Decreased Performance or Cognitive Difficulties**: Overstimulation can make it harder for them to concentrate, process information, or perform well academically.

Let Them Be Creative

It is a well-known fact that these children are more in tune with their creative side, whether it's through writing stories, making art, or performing a musical piece. They also love to spend time in nature, as it makes them feel calm. So, while you should ensure that they focus on their academics, you should also let them explore their creative side. Encourage them to pursue their passions and interests instead of shackling them to the confines of what society believes to be academic success.

Break Large Tasks into Manageable Chunks.

Complex projects, activities, and performances can be quite overwhelming for an HSC, as they cannot take in too many things at once. This causes overstimulation, which then takes away their ability to work or focus. Instead of expecting your child to absorb everything right away like a sponge, break down big projects into smaller, more manageable chunks of work that you think they can handle. Make sure that you set specific goals along the way so that as they complete each step, they feel a sense of accomplishment and are motivated to keep going. For example, if your HSC is working on a big project, you could outline smaller tasks such as conducting research, organizing information, creating an outline, drafting sections, and revising. By breaking it down into these manageable steps, your child can tackle each one at their own pace, feeling a sense of achievement after completing each stage. Similarly, for performances or presentations, you can help them break down the preparation process. This may involve practicing specific sections, working on stage presence or delivery, and gradually integrating all elements until they feel comfortable and confident.

Give Positive Feedback

Highly sensitive kids are not only deeply aware of the criticism they are given but also of the praise they get. They love to be praised and appreciated for their efforts and abilities more than anything. Positive reinforcement is something that works wonders for highly sensitive children, especially if they have a hard time accomplishing their goals. So, whenever they're studying or working on a project, remember to give them positive feedback. Instead of focusing on the end result, you should focus on their progress and how much effort they're putting in and praise them for this effort. This will encourage them to keep going even if they're making mistakes.

Another effective approach is to assign them the scores they genuinely deserve. Awarding them a high score that accurately reflects their accomplishment reinforces their belief in their abilities and recognizes their hard work. In addition, consider physically acknowledging their achievements. You can do this by stamping their work with a seal of approval, placing a sticker on their paper, or using other visual cues to signify their success. These small gestures can have a powerful impact, providing them with a tangible reminder of their accomplishments.

Teach Them Problem-Solving Skills

A common problem that HSCs face academically is that they get overwhelmed by different situations and are unable to find a solution. As a parent, teach them how to effectively solve a problem while dealing with their stress and anxiety. Problem-solving skills and other executive functioning skills are essential for any kid, especially HSCs. Not only will they benefit from these learned skills in their schoolwork, but also in their adult lives. Many parents make the mistake of solving their kids' problems for them instead of even giving them a chance to try.

However, this is not the correct way to go about this and will only make their abilities worse. The best way to help them is to give them the tools and techniques to solve their problems so they can do it themselves instead of relying on you or someone else. Here are some instructions you can share with your highly sensitive child to teach them about problem-solving:

· The first step is to identify the problem at hand. Ask your child to tell you the problem or say it out loud.

· Next, they should come up with five different solutions. Initially, you can help them with this and brainstorm the solutions together. Let them know that not all the solutions need to be good. If they're still struggling, you can help them out by giving some ideas of your own. Never judge their ideas or belittle them.

· Now, analyze each solution by comparing its pros and cons. Ask your kid to participate in each step of the process and discuss the solutions in detail. They should understand the negative and positive consequences each solution could have.

· Once you've evaluated and compared the solutions, ask your child to pick the best one. Avoid making this choice for them, and instead encourage them to make it themselves.

· Test out the solution. If it doesn't work out, there are always more solutions you can try.

Teach Them Time Management

Highly sensitive children can easily become stressed, especially when faced with multiple tasks and responsibilities. The early years of school can be particularly challenging for them. If you want to support your child during this time, teaching them time management skills is key. Learning how to follow a schedule and be consistent with it can make a significant difference. The good news is that most sensitive kids actually enjoy having a routine, so it shouldn't be too difficult to implement. Effective time management skills also prevent the development of detrimental habits like procrastination.

You should guide your child toward avoiding this habit by demonstrating the value of handling and completing tasks promptly. Encourage them to finish their homework and extracurricular activities on the same day without unnecessary delay. You can play a vital role in teaching your child time management by setting a positive example. Show them how you manage your own work schedule and maintain a sense of organization. By doing so, you help your child understand the importance of managing time effectively and demonstrate practical strategies for doing so.

Learning Styles

Every child has a different learning style that is unique to their personality, their interests, and their cognitive understanding. For HSCs, if you try to teach them through a learning style that does not align with their personality, it'll be as effective as trying to fit a square peg into a round hole. On the other hand, if you find out which learning style works best with your child, you'll be able to play to their strengths and considerably improve their learning process. There are four main types of learning styles:

- Visual
- Auditory
- Tactile
- Kinesthetic

The best way to understand your child's learning style is through careful observation of their actions, interests, and preferences. Pay attention to how they engage with information, and you will soon figure out their learning process. It's essential to shift your focus from what your child may not yet be doing, especially if they have developmental delays, and instead concentrate on their strengths and favorite activities. Talk to family members and teachers to see how your child learns and retains knowledge. Ask yourself the following questions:

- What types of toys does your child gravitate towards? Do they prefer quiet, solitary activities or ones that involve a lot of movement?
- Do they enjoy reading books and engaging in artistic activities such as drawing or painting? Do they prefer visual demonstrations over verbal instructions?
- Is your child energetic and drawn to more active and physical pursuits?
- Does your child exhibit an interest in numbers and patterns?

By actively exploring these aspects of your child's interests and preferences, you can gain valuable insights into their learning style. This understanding can help you tailor educational experiences to their needs, promote engagement, and enhance their overall motivation for learning.

11

PARENTING SELF-CARE AND SUPPORT

A parent can easily overlook the emotional labor invested in raising a highly sensitive child. Having responsibility for a child who has very particular needs can be a lot. As parents, it is easy to neglect your health to ensure your child is cared for. The natural desire to put yourself last is often detrimental. However, this is not in the best interest of either a parent or a child. Consider the analogy of an airplane oxygen mask. Staff on a plane advise parents that in the event of an emergency when oxygen masks drop, the parent should put the mask on first. For a parent to put a mask on before they make sure their child is okay seems counterintuitive; however, if the parent passes out or is injured, they will not be able to care for the child. Therefore, it is in the child's best interest for the parent to make sure that they are okay first.

Considering how demanding raising a highly sensitive child can be, for a parent to be in the most appropriate mental and physical space for effective self-care is essential. Many are not accustomed to treating themselves with the same compassion they treat others with. As social creatures, it is easy for people to neglect themselves. It is even easier to neglect yourself when there is a perception that your child needs more care and attention. Internalizing the reality that taking care of yourself does not mean taking away from your child is essential for present parenting. Falling into the trap of stress-induced burnout is disastrous for both the parent and the child. Therefore, self-care is central to optimizing relationship frameworks that create the safety that a highly sensitive child needs.

The Stressful Reality of Parenting a Highly Sensitive Child

Sometimes parents are tempted to push down all their emotions and burdens because of the additional care that comes with raising a highly sensitive child. The problem is that these negative experiences and feelings do not really go away. Much like a pipe that is overflowing with pressurized liquid, it is only a matter of time before cracks and leaks become uncontrollable. Unaddressed stress can cause cardiovascular disorders, mental issues like memory loss, and an impaired immune system (Yaribeygi et al., 2017). Stress is a healthy hormonal response internally, that ensures that balance is maintained within the complexities of the body. However, stress becomes detrimental when it is prolonged. Therefore, mindfully taking steps to reduce your stress responses when parenting a highly sensitive child will ensure that your health is in a condition that allows you to respond to the needs of your child.

A certain level of societal guilt is perpetuated in terms of admitting struggles with parenting and nurturing. Nobody wants to be perceived as incapable of meeting their child's needs. The parenting stakes are high, even more so when caring for a highly sensitive child. Traumatizing a child is a reality that no mindful parent wants to embody. Parenting any child comes with an endless laundry list of concerns, never mind the specialized needs that are necessary to consider for a highly sensitive child. There is a certain level of unpredictability in a highly sensitive child's responses. What can seem like a fun family outing for many could be the perfect breeding ground for an emotional breakdown. These additional concerns that many parents overlook and the excessive contemplation before going anywhere or doing anything could really take a toll on your well-being.

On top of all the considerations and adjustments you make when parenting a highly sensitive child, there may be judgment from other parents who do not understand. The emotional swings and episodes that are often part and parcel of one's journey could be judged as a lack of discipline or as bad parenting. As much as you try to ignore these kinds of comments and ignorant attitudes, the social nature of human beings sometimes internalizes these criticisms as reality. The combination of internal turmoil and external pressure create a melting pot of extremes that could easily derail a parent if it is allowed to take over. Then the guilt of your child being the source of the stress is just the added spice needed to throw you over the edge. Tackling the guilt and showing yourself love and affection does not come without intentional practice. Just like it is necessary for a parent to tune into how their child functions through proactive research and work, one needs to tap into themselves in a similar way.

Raising a highly sensitive child requires a lot of empathy and compassion. One of the keys to sustaining yourself in this parenting journey is directing some of that compassion inward. The love that a highly sensitive child deserves is the same kind of love you also need. Before a parent mentally and physically destroys themselves by neglecting their own needs, there must be systems in place to address the realities of raising a highly sensitive child. Your child can only be whole if you are whole. Therefore, meeting your child's needs effectively means meeting your own needs on the physical, emotional, and psychological levels.

The Importance of Self-Care

Self-care is one of the most overused terms in the current discourse. It is easy to dismiss self-care as a buzzword for social media influencers who need an excuse to sip pina coladas on a tropical beach. However, when you dive deep into the concept of self-care, it becomes apparent that it is essential to become fully actualized in the role of a conscious parent. A child does not know a parent's limits, especially when the child is a highly sensitive individual who can be extremely demanding at times. A child is not going to let up on the gas pedal because, more often than not, your child will not pick up the cues that you are at your breaking point. Therefore, you must take your self-care into your own hands. Self-care practices could help parents to maintain positivity, focus and to restore their energy. Taking care of yourself is not selfish; it is the only way that you can truly fulfill the high-stress position of being a parent.

Neglecting yourself is not the righteous endeavor that it idealistically seems in your mind. Not creating room for it breeds resentment, resulting in negative behaviors toward your child. As much as a child views a parent as superhuman, taking on this impenetrable role will end in disaster. Self-care is about acknowledging that you have limitations. It is in these limitations that growth and development take place. The world's greatest athletes have an off-season, and they consistently train to be the best. Therefore, even the super-parent needs to take time to heal themselves. A lot of internal wounds will develop in the process of raising a child. These wounds must be cleaned and bandaged, or they will fester and become infected. Imagine driving a car at its maximum speed every day without changing its oil, refilling the water, or servicing it. The same car that takes you from point A to point B will break down in the middle of a shady neighborhood when you need it to work the most.

The unique needs of these children require parents to be fully engaged. So, to ensure you are at your best, refueling stations, i.e., self-care time outs, must be established. These practices can take a variety of forms that are adaptable to each individual. One of the primary principles of self-care is establishing an identity outside of being connected to your child. This could take the form of getting into a personal hobby or connecting with friends and family. Self-care doesn't need to be anything too drastic or complicated. Taking care of yourself can be as simple as taking a daily walk for a few minutes or listening to music alone. Mental peace of mind can come from embracing something that one finds enjoyment in and just allowing yourself to be immersed in that activity or practice.

Many find solace in spiritual practices or in connecting with a higher power. You don't necessarily have to be religious to find something that gives life meaning outside of caring for your child. Self-care comes from diversification and embracing the fact that there are a multitude of facets that make up your being. Parents of a highly sensitive child need to find that individualized fuel or that personalized rest station so that the energy for connecting with your child can be stoked effectively. The desire to take the back seat in your own life because of your child's needs is tempting due to the indescribable love that parents have, but self-care is so necessary that this urge must be fought to carve out the time to connect with self.

Setting Boundaries and Building Support Systems

It is impossible for a parent to always be available for their child. Although a highly sensitive child may require more time and effort, it is still essential for a parent to take time for themselves. This is why setting boundaries is necessary. A parent will always be available to a child in emergencies and when the need arises, but boundaries provide structure. One such boundary is time because dedicating all your time to interacting with and worrying about your child is a surefire way to burn out. Taking time out of the day or the week where you can engage in self-centered activities is a healthy habit to build. These kinds of boundaries will craft some independence in a child who will then not be completely reliant on a parent at all times and will give you the distance needed to rejuvenate.

Creating these boundaries is best done with a support system. Maybe there is someone who can care for your child when you are not available, like family or friends. There is a reason for the saying, "It takes a village to raise a child." Having someone close to the family and the child who is aware of the needs of a highly sensitive child could be a life-changing resource. Reaching out to friends and family can be difficult, especially if you are filled with your own anxieties, but if there are trusted members within your circle, it is advisable to make use of these relationships. This doesn't mean that your child is going to be dumped by someone uneducated on the needs of a highly sensitive child. Being open to communication and asking for help does not demean the important role you play in a child's life. Sometimes parents can develop toxic independence induced by fear responses. Overcoming this fear of reaching out opens the possibilities for new healthy experiences between you and your child.

Friends and family can be a great help, but sometimes a support system of people who understand what it is like to be a parent of a highly sensitive child is even better assistance. Reaching out to online groups or forums could be a great avenue to discover new tips or to share experiences. The beauty of the online space is that communities of people who once felt isolated and alone are now able to connect. The same is true for parents of highly sensitive children. Therefore, connecting with people who intimately understand the details of raising a highly sensitive child is incredibly reassuring. Furthermore, you'll find groups or individuals in your area through the internet. Building a community around people with similar experiences is psychologically and emotionally beneficial. You do not need to meet up with anyone or ask too much of strangers. The act of communicating with people who understand is enough to make a substantial difference in your well-being.

Seeking Professional Help

A strong support system in the form of family, friends, and even online relationships can be very helpful, but sometimes you need additional assistance that can only come from a professional. Well-meaning people will always try to provide advice, but they could be leading parents astray. When consulting a professional, you can be confident data and studies inform their opinion. Consulting a professional gives you the tools in your unique context to prosper. Focus on mental health has come to the forefront of popular conversation in recent years. The stigma attached to seeking out a psychologist is dying. This progress away from misunderstanding the profession of psychology has opened many doors. Therefore, now is the perfect time to seek professional help because societal attitudes toward mental health have begun shifting. Furthermore, a professional will have a deeper insight into the mindset and perceptions of someone that is easily stimulated.

Individual Therapy

One-on-one counseling lets you dive deeper into what causes the emotional and mental stress that often manifests through physical ailments. There is a misconception that therapy is where someone goes for advice. This is very seldom the case. The core role of a therapist is to walk the client through different scenarios and exercises to provide an individual with the tools to come to more informed conclusions. With individual therapy, you'll slow down and analyze the automatic responses and decisions you make.

By taking the time to navigate yourself internally, you'll come to understand what influences the decisions you make as a parent in a way that can bring the most out of your child. As a parent, you are in a role of authority, so having the correct information about yourself and your circumstances allows for the leadership position to be mindfully navigated. Addressing your own biases and issues could help you avoid perpetuating any trauma that may have been inherited from previous generations. In this way, a road to understanding is paved with the self-care of mental work.

Family Therapy

Family therapy allows counselors to create an environment of alliance within a family. As a neutral party, the therapist can mediate and allows all individuals to work through their emotions. By establishing therapeutic alliances which allow for separate and joint sessions, a family is able to work through a variety of issues to both address and prevent relational trauma (Gilson and Abela, 2021). Even though family therapy is not only focused on self, but also still a form of self-care because it helps establish the boundaries and protocols that create a healthy home environment.

Taking a unified approach to self-care in a therapeutic setting could be revolutionary in working out certain kinks that are preventing you from creating the best home environment for you and your child. There are certain blind spots that are often only revealed with the help of a therapist. The professional setting of therapy can give the guidance needed to minimize melt-downs from overstimulation while giving you the tools to address issues related to high sensitivity with compassion and patience. Group therapy allows for joint self-care, which is advantageous to strengthening familial bonds and helping you and your child prosper.

CONCLUSION

By now, you know that raising a highly sensitive child can be challenging. Although they have been blessed with a set of special gifts that can benefit them in different areas of their lives, it can also overwhelm them and raise their anxiety. For your child to survive in our noisy world, a peaceful environment is vital, together with plenty of understanding from parents and caregivers.

Understandably, you have many questions because you want to support your child and give them the best care. This book collected all your concerns and provided effective strategies you could easily apply to make your little one's life easier.

The book began by answering the number one question on your mind, "Is my child highly sensitive?" It introduced the concept of high sensitivity with scientific research and psychological theories and the main characteristics of a highly sensitive child.

Your child can't regulate their emotions without emotional intelligence. The book provided helpful techniques to foster this quality in your child so they could have a better understanding of their emotions. It also included tips on how to make your home a safe haven for your child so they can relax their mind after bouts of overstimulation and intense emotions.

Parents should foster effective communication skills in their highly sensitive children from a young age. The book presented several methods to use to address their needs during conflict or stressful situations.

Since highly sensitive children suffer from anxiety, many relaxation techniques were included that your child could easily use in their daily lives. You can't be with your child 24/7, so you need to prepare them to face the world on their own. The book included empowering techniques your child could use during social situations so they could confidently interact with others and establish relationships.

The book then explained what elements to consider when looking for a school for your highly sensitive child and the type of support they need while pursuing their education.

Your child won't grow out of their sensitivity which was why the book explained how you could handle your child during each developmental stage of their life. It also discussed the social challenges your child faces and the qualities you should foster in them to improve their social and communication skills.

It then moved on to explain how you could create a learning environment that accommodates your child's needs. The last chapter focused on the parents and how they shouldn't neglect themselves and make time every day to practice self-care.

Be patient with your child and understand that they can't control how they feel. Remember, you are their teacher and their guide, so give them constant love and support. Keep this book with you, and always go back to it whenever you face any challenges with your highly sensitive child.

REFERENCES

Humphries, L. (2016, July 13). 8 reasons being highly sensitive is A gift in disguise. Lifehack. https://www.lifehack.org/424779/8-reasons-being-highly-sensitive-is-a-gift-in-disguise

Julian. (2022, May 18). Highly sensitive children: Canaries in the Coal Mine. Teaching Heart Institute. https://teachingheartinstitute.com/highly-sensitive-child-canaries-in-the-coal-mine/

What Does It Mean to Be a Highly Sensitive Person? (n.d.). Embry Women's Health. https://embrywomenshealth.com/what-does-it-mean-to-be-a-highly-sensitive-person/

Scott, E. (n.d.). What Is a Highly Sensitive Person (HSP)? Verywell Mind. https://www.verywellmind.com/highly-sensitive-persons-traits-that-create-more-stress-4126393

Pluess, M. (2021, November 26). Here's Everything Researchers Know About High Sensitivity as of 2021. Sensitive Refuge - Your Sensitivity Is Your Greatest Strength. https://highlysensitiverefuge.com/heres-everything-researchers-know-about-high-sensitivity-as-of-2021/

Sheppard, S. (n.d.). How Dopamine Influences Your Mental Health. Verywell Mind. https://www.verywellmind.com/what-is-dopamine-5185621

Granneman, J., & Sólo, A. (2023, March 4). Kids who do these 12 things have "highly sensitive" brains—why parenting experts say it's an "advantage." CNBC. https://www.cnbc.com/2023/03/04/parenting-experts-signs-your-kid-has-a-highly-sensitive-brain-why-neuroscientists-says-its-an-advantage.html

5 steps to nurture emotional intelligence in your child. (n.d.). Ahaparenting.com. https://www.ahaparenting.com/read/steps-to-encourage

10 traits of highly sensitive children. (n.d.). Psychology Today. https://www.psychologytoday.com/intl/blog/zero-six/202202/10-traits-highly-sensitive-children

Amy Morin, L. (2018, February 7). 6 parenting strategies for raising emotionally intelligent kids. Verywell Family. https://www.verywellfamily.com/tips-for-raising-an-emotionally-intelligent-child-4157946

Callarman, S. (2020, June 8). The unique emotional intelligence of highly sensitive people. Sensitive Refuge - Your Sensitivity Is Your Greatest Strength. https://highlysensitiverefuge.com/emotional-intelligence/

Donna Volpitta, E. (2019, October 16). Build emotional intelligence in children.

REFERENCES

Understood. https://www.understood.org/en/articles/6-tips-for-helping-your-child-build-emotional-intelligence

Kendra Cherry, M. (2006, September 8). Emotional intelligence: How we perceive, evaluate, express, and control emotions. Verywell Mind. https://www.verywellmind.com/what-is-emotional-intelligence-2795423

Melody Wilding, L. (2017, June 13). Being sensitive is a superpower -- here are 5 ways to use it. Psych Central. https://psychcentral.com/blog/being-sensitive-is-a-superpower-heres-5-ways-to-use-it

MindTools. (n.d.). Mindtools.com. https://www.mindtools.com/ab4u682/emotional-intelligence

Samson, R. (2021, September 13). Emotion coaching and the highly sensitive child. The Gottman Institute. https://www.gottman.com/blog/emotion-coaching-and-the-highly-sensitive-child/

Supporting your child's emotional regulation: Effective strategies for parents. (n.d.). Blacknyellow.In. https://blacknyellow.in/blog/emotional_regulation

Van Der Wagen, L. (2008). Emotional Intelligence. In Customer Service Intelligence (pp. 33–46). Elsevier.

Guest User. (2023, March 8). 20 tips for how to understand and parent your highly sensitive child. Little Otter. https://www.littleotterhealth.com/blog/highly-sensitive-child

Kids, P. (2021, June 29). How to support your highly sensitive child. PBS KIDS for Parents. https://www.pbs.org/parents/thrive/how-to-support-your-highly-sensitive-child

Li, P. (2022, January 17). How to parent and build confidence in your highly sensitive child. Parenting For Brain. https://www.parentingforbrain.com/highly-sensitive-child/

Morin, A. (2013, May 6). 8 discipline strategies for parenting a sensitive child. Verywell Family. https://www.verywellfamily.com/parenting-a-sensitive-child-8-discipline-strategies-1094942

Pluess, M. (2020, May 9). Parenting quality and sensitive children. Sensitivity Research. https://sensitivityresearch.com/parenting-quality-and-sensitive-children/

Russell, L. (2023, May 31). Parenting strategies for your highly sensitive child. They Are The Future. https://www.theyarethefuture.co.uk/highly-sensitive-child-parenting-strategies/

Smit, A. W. (2016, August 31). 10 practical and fun tips for living with (high) sensitive children. Ankewebersmit.com. https://ankewebersmit.com/en/10-practical-and-fun-tips-for-living-with-high-sensitive-children/

Chang, C. (2021, March 30). How to help your sensitive kid handle an overwhelming world. Parents. https://www.parents.com/toddlers-preschoolers/development/behavioral/expert-tips-to-help-your-sensitive-child-navigate-an-overwhelming-world/

REFERENCES

Friendship circle / resources. (n.d.). Friendshipcircle.org. http://www.friendship-circle.org/blog/2017/08/08/how-to-talk-to-your-sensitive-child

Li, P. (2022, January 17). How to parent and build confidence in your highly sensitive child. Parenting For Brain. https://www.parentingforbrain.com/highly-sensitive-child/

Morin, A. (2013, May 6). 8 discipline strategies for parenting a sensitive child. Verywell Family. https://www.verywellfamily.com/parenting-a-sensitive-child-8-discipline-strategies-1094942

Peterson, T. J. (n.d.). The best parenting strategies for highly sensitive children. Healthyplace.com. https://www.healthyplace.com/parenting/parenting-skills-strategies/the-best-parenting-strategies-for-highly-sensitive-children

Sherred, L. (2020, September 8). How communication issues can impact a child's social and emotional well-being. Expressable. https://www.expressable.com/learning-center/social-emotional-academic/how-communication-issues-can-impact-a-childs-social-and-emotional-well-being

Amy Morin, L. (2019, February 25). 15 coping strategies for kids. Verywell Family. https://www.verywellfamily.com/coping-skills-for-kids-4586871

Brian, H. (2023, February 21). Five tips to manage your stress. Mayo Clinic Health System. https://www.mayoclinichealthsystem.org/hometown-health/speaking-of-health/5-tips-to-manage-stress

Corliss, J. (2022, February 2). Six relaxation techniques to reduce stress. Harvard Health. https://www.health.harvard.edu/mind-and-mood/six-relaxation-techniques-to-reduce-stress

GoodTherapy. (n.d.). Goodtherapy.org. https://www.goodtherapy.org/blog/5-things-that-help-a-child-with-high-sensitivity-and-anxiety-070914

Paulson, D. (2021, August 31). 9 tools for helping your child manage anxiety. Mayo Clinic Health System. https://www.mayoclinichealthsystem.org/hometown-health/speaking-of-health/9-tools-for-helping-your-child-manage-anxiety

Relaxation techniques: Try these steps to reduce stress. (2022, April 28). Mayo Clinic. https://www.mayoclinic.org/healthy-lifestyle/stress-management/in-depth/relaxation-technique/art-20045368

Sutton, J. (2022, January 2). 7 best grounding tools and techniques to manage anxiety. Positivepsychology.com. https://positivepsychology.com/grounding-tools-techniques/

Chang, C. (2021, March 30). How to help your sensitive kid handle an overwhelming world. Parents. https://www.parents.com/toddlers-preschoolers/development/behavioral/expert-tips-to-help-your-sensitive-child-navigate-an-overwhelming-world/

Pace, A. (2018, January 30). How to empower and celebrate your sensitive son. Parenting From The Heart. https://parentingfromtheheartblog.com/sensitive-son-man-up/

7 tips to help A highly sensitive child flourish in school. (2015, August 26). Happysensitivekids.com; amandavmulligen. https://happysensitivekids.com/2015/08/7-tips-to-help-a-highly-sensitive-child-flourish-in-school/

8 Questions to Ask when Choosing a School for your Sensitive Child. (2019, February 25). The Highly Sensitive Child. https://www.thehighlysensitivechild.com/8-questions-to-ask-when-choosing-a-school-for-your-sensitive-child/

Day, N. (2022, February 2). The best way to support highly sensitive kids in school. Sensitive Refuge - Your Sensitivity Is Your Greatest Strength. https://highlysensitiverefuge.com/how-to-support-highly-sensitive-kids-in-school/

Eanes, R. (n.d.). 5 strengths of sensitive kids. Creative Child Magazine. https://www.creativechild.com/articles/view/5-strengths-of-sensitive-kids

Paul, M. (2022, March 14). The Role of School in child's life and their education. Orchids. https://www.orchidsinternationalschool.com/blog/child-learning/role-of-school/

What would make school perfect for your highly sensitive child? (2017, January 31). Happysensitivekids.com; amandavmulligen. https://happysensitivekids.com/2017/01/the-perfect-school-for-a-highly-sensitive-child/

Wirz, G. (2020, June 25). "Sensitive children shouldn't have to learn in the wrong environment." BOLD. https://bold.expert/sensitive-children-shouldnt-have-to-learn-in-the-wrong-environment/

Chang, C. (n.d.). How to Help Your Sensitive Kid Handle an Overwhelming World. Parents. https://www.parents.com/toddlers-preschoolers/development/behavioral/expert-tips-to-help-your-sensitive-child-navigate-an-overwhelming-world/

Russell, L. (2023, May 31). Parenting Strategies For Your Highly Sensitive Child. They Are The Future. https://www.theyarethefuture.co.uk/highly-sensitive-child-parenting-strategies/

Nasamran, A. (2021, March 1). Highly Sensitive Child Parenting Strategies. Atlas Psychology. https://www.atlaspsychologycollective.com/blog/highly-sensitive-child-parenting-strategies

Yulia. (2021, September 30). Parenting A Highly Sensitive Child. Mighty Kids. https://mightykidsacademy.com/parenting-a-highly-sensitive-child/

junecao. (2021, February 4). How to Help your Highly Sensitive Teen to Manage Stress. Mind Connections. https://mindconnectionsnyc.com/how-to-help-your-highly-sensitive-teen-to-manage-stress/

Gongala, S. (2015, March 18). 12 signs of A highly sensitive child and tips to help them MomJunction. https://www.momjunction.com/articles/parenting-tips-to-handle-a-highly-sensitive-child_00336867/

The ultimate guide to friendships and. (2017, November 10). The Highly Sensitive Child. https://www.thehighlysensitivechild.com/the-ultimate-guide-to-friendships-and-the-highly-sensitive-child/

Li, P. (2022, January 17). How to parent and build confidence in your highly sensitive child. Parenting For Brain. https://www.parentingforbrain.com/highly-sensitive-child/

7 tips to help A highly sensitive child flourish in school. (2015, August 26). Happysensitivekids.com; amandavmulligen. https://happysensitivekids.com/2015/08/7-tips-to-help-a-highly-sensitive-child-flourish-in-school/

Children's learning styles. (2020, March 9). AbilityPath. https://ability-path.org/ap-resources/childrens-learning-styles/

How to accommodate different learning styles in the classroom. (2021, July 8). Allison Academy. https://www.allisonacademy.com/students/learning/learning-styles/how-to-accommodate-different-learning-styles-in-the-classroom/

Lynch, M. (2023, May 15). How to parent and build confidence in your highly sensitive child. The Edvocate. https://www.theedadvocate.org/how-to-parent-and-build-confidence-in-your-highly-sensitive-child/

Scott, S. (2023, June 28). 7 strategies for parenting a highly sensitive child. Happier Human; Steve Scott. https://www.happierhuman.com/highly-sensitive-child/

van Mulligen, A. (2021, September 8). School has started. Here's how to advocate for your sensitive child. Sensitive Refuge - Your Sensitivity Is Your Greatest Strength. https://highlysensitiverefuge.com/how-to-advocate-for-your-sensitive-child-at-school/

Gilson, M. L., & Abela, A. (2021). The therapeutic alliance with parents and their children working through a relational trauma in the family. Contemporary Family Therapy, 43(4), 343–358. https://doi.org/10.1007/s10591-021-09607-4

Ginsburg, K. R. (2014). The importance of self-care for parents. In Reaching Teens (pp. 315–318). American Academy of Pediatrics.https://www.psychologytoday.com/za/blog/adolescents-explained/202107/the-importance-self-care-parents

Yaribeygi, H., Panahi, Y., Sahraei, H., Johnston, T. P., & Sahebkar, A. (2017). The impact of stress on body function: A review. EXCLI Journal, 16, 1057–1072. https://doi.org/10.17179/excli2017-480

Made in United States
North Haven, CT
02 February 2024